CRACKING

THE

WALL

Women in Higher Education Administration

Edited by
Patricia Turner Mitchell, Ph.D.

College and University Personnel Association

The College and University Personnel Association (CUPA) is an international network of more than 5,000 human resource administrators representing 1,700 colleges, universities and others interested in the advancement of the human resource profession.

The primary goal of the Association is to promote the effective management and development of human resources in higher education. CUPA works to achieve this goal by providing a forum for the exchange of ideas through annual conventions, workshops, and seminars that allow members and others interested in the topic of human resource management to meet one-on-one and to increase their professional development through informative educational sessions. The Association also conducts research and analysis on administrative and faculty salaries, benefits, and other topics through surveys and special study reports. Another important member service provided by CUPA is the publication of periodicals, monographs, books and videotapes.

Typesetting and Cover Design by C. David Hopkins, CUPA
Cover Photograph by Dr. Laurence Bishop, University of San Francisco

© Copyright 1993 by
The College and University Personnel Association
1233 20th Street, NW, Suite 301
Washington, DC 20036-1250
(202) 429-0311

ISBN: 1-878240-21-8

To Larry, my husband;
to my daughter Candyce;
to my two sons Jason and Jeremy;
to my parents James and Ruth Turner.

Contents

Preface

This book is about change—change that is personal as well as institutional. It is about change that has already occurred, and change that is still needed if women are to be full participants in higher education and the leadership of higher education institutions.

Through the publication of this book, the College and University Personnel Association, an organization serving the human resource needs of colleges and universities nationwide, has given additional recognition to the importance of the topic of women in higher education administration. Editor Patricia Mitchell and the contributing authors provide the reader a context in which to understand where women are today in gaining access to positions of leadership in higher education. The topic is approached from a variety of perspectives—historical, sociological, political, psychological and personal.

The authors consist of women in a variety of professional positions throughout the academy. The chapters include research findings, descriptive reports and personal observations. The reader will learn from those who have studied women's progress in higher education administrative careers as well as those who have attained leadership positions and who have been successful in implementing change strategies at both the personal and organizational level. The book gives significant treatment to the topic of career paths in higher education, including both traditional and non-traditional routes to achieving leadership positions. There is also extensive coverage of strategies for enhancing advancement opportunities.

This book will be an asset to women who are interested in entry or advancement in higher education administration. It is also a resource for all higher education administrators who are in the position to mentor and to assist in the advancement of talented people. Those charged with responsibility for developing the human resources of colleges and universities will benefit from the discussion of organizational barriers that must be removed if women are to become full participants in providing leadership to institutions of higher education.

It is hoped that the reader will be further enlightened about the need for greater inclusion of women in higher education administration positions and informed as how this can be accomplished by the strategies and recommendations included in this book. Lastly, it is hoped that the reader will be inspired to action, not only to widen the "crack in the wall," but to help move toward the day when walls (and ceilings) no longer exist to constrain the development of skills and the expression of talents of any member within the higher education community.

Judith A. Anderson, Ph.D.
California State University, Fullerton

Acknowledgements

As the editor of *Cracking the Wall: Women in Higher Education Administration*, I would like to express my deep gratitude and appreciation to several people who contributed to the preparation of this book.

- Colleagues who wrote the manuscript for the book: Judith Anderson, Del Anderson, Deborah LeBlanc, Bonnie Jones, Lindalee Ausejo, Fay Bower, Joyce Owens, Mary Flynn, Karen Johnson, Jean Treiman, Carol Harter, Anita Harrow, Rebecca Warner, and Lois DeFleur;

- Father John P. Schlegel for writing the postscript;

- Larry Bishop for helping design the cover for the book;

- Lourie W. Reichenberg and the outstanding publications department at CUPA;

- Dan Julius for being my mentor, friend, and valued colleague;

- The School of Education of the University of San Francisco for giving me the opportunity to develop and teach the course "Women in Management;"

- My colleagues in the School of Education for their support;

- Lindalee Ausejo and Sister Kevina Keating for their counsel and for sharing creative thinking on women's issues;

- My parents, James and Ruth Turner, for encouraging me always to do my best;

- My children, Candyce, Jason and Jeremy for their love and understanding; and

- Last, but not least, my husband, Larry, for his words of encouragement, his love and support while working on this project.

CUPA Publications and Research Advisory Board

About the Editor

PATRICIA TURNER MITCHELL is a faculty member in the School of Education at the University of San Francisco. Dr. Mitchell earned her B.S. degree from Morgan State College, Baltimore, Maryland; her M.S. degree from Southern Illinois University, Carbondale, and her Ph.D. in Educational Administration and Higher Education from The Catholic University of America in Washington, D.C. She has delivered papers and made presentations around the country on women's issues and sexual harassment. She has served as a consultant in the area of women in management for several corporations and has conducted research in the area of managerial traits, gender issues, and the psychology of women. She currently teaches a Women in Management course at the University of San Francisco.

Introduction

*"I gain strength, courage and confidence by every
experience in which I must stop and look fear in the
face...
I say to myself, I've lived through this and can take
the next thing that comes along...
We must do the things we think we cannot do."*

Eleanor Roosevelt

These words of Eleanor Roosevelt echo the underlying motivation of
many women who have made a crack in the brick wall at our colleges
and universities through advancement into higher education management. They are saying to themselves "we must do the things we think
we cannot do." They have been faced with obstacles, but many have
forged ahead and have continued to make a small crack in the brick
wall that has impeded many from advancement.

Twelve years ago, I developed a course entitled, "Women in Management," for the School of Education's doctoral program in Organizational Leadership at the University of San Francisco. The purpose
of the course was to offer, in a seminar setting, an exploration of selected
aspects of management as they related to women. The course mainly
focused on women in corporate America. Each semester some of the
same issues resurfaced and we kept talking about those barriers that
for years have impeded women's advancement. One of the textbooks
that I used in the class was *Breaking the Glass Ceiling: Can Women
Reach the Top of America's Largest Corporations?* by Ann Morrison
and the Center for Creative Leadership. The book is based on a three
year study of 76 women executives in America's largest manufacturing
and service companies. This book motivated me to investigate the
situation on our college and university campuses.

For the past two years, the course has taken a slightly different focus
with more emphasis being placed on women in higher education
administration. What I discovered was that the same barriers that have
impeded women from climbing the corporate ladder have also stopped
them from climbing the ivory tower ladder.

After conducting an extensive search, I found numerous journal
articles dealing with many issues facing women in higher education
administration, but very few books that have attempted to put these
issues together.

Is the woman administrator for the 21st Century androgynous?
Are there certain myths and stereotypes that we have of women

administrators? Do we have the same expectations for women as we do for men? Do women behave differently than men administrators? Do women administrators make better use of the informal organization? Do woman administrators have unique behavioral traits? Do women administrators ask for special favors? Why are women not advancing in administrative positions? These are just a few of the many questions regarding women in college and university management that remain unanswered as we approach the 21st Century.

While the number of women in administrative positions has increased, we have only made a crack in the brick wall. As a matter of fact, it is only a hairline fracture. Women are still unrepresented in many of the key administrative positions in colleges and universities. According to the American Council on Education, only 328 of more than 3,000 college presidents are women. *The Catalyst* reports that 44.5 percent of the work force is composed of women and 36 percent of all management positions are filled by women.

Once women do achieve administrative positions, there are other issues that become burdensome or stumbling blocks for advancement to even higher levels.

This book, *Cracking the Wall: Women in Higher Education Administration*, is a compilation of well-documented and personally informed papers written by women from across the nation, on issues and barriers facing women.

It is hoped that this book will raise your consciousness level; alert you to the barriers and stumbling blocks that continue to confront women in academia as they attempt to climb the ivory tower's ladder to success; and offer specific strategies for dealing with and overcoming these barriers.

Patricia Turner Mitchell

ABSTRACT

This chapter will examine the effects of educational background, faculty experience, sponsorship, and entry position on the current administrative positions of a cross-section of senior level administrators at U.S. institutions of higher education.

Data for this study were collected via a mail survey of senior academic administrators. Initially, 800 administrators with the title of Dean or above were randomly selected from the Higher Education Directory, and sent a questionnaire. We made no restrictions on the type of institution, and therefore questionnaires were sent to senior administrators at universities, colleges, community colleges, and technical schools throughout the United States. Two waves of the survey were sent, with a reminder postcard sent between the two waves. Nine surveys were returned undeliverable. Completed surveys were returned by 394 respondents producing a response rate of 50 percent. Using information from the *Higher Education Directory* we compared respondents to nonrespondents on gender (using name), position title, and type of institution (university, college, etc.). We found no statistically significant differences between respondents and nonrespondents on these variables.

Chapter One

Career Paths of Women in Higher Education Administration

Rebecca Warner and Lois B. DeFleur

Although women have made progress over the last 15 years in obtaining senior level administrative positions, these gains have not been distributed across all types of institutions or departments within institutions. In 1987, approximately 22 percent of administrators at state and land-grant institutions were women, yet women represented only about 3 percent of presidents and 15 percent of chief academic officers and deans. A more recent analysis completed by the American Council on Education is somewhat encouraging in its findings that the rate at which women were appointed presidents at colleges and

REBECCA WARNER is an Assistant Professor of Sociology at Oregon State University. Since receiving her Ph.D. from Washington State University in 1985 she has focused her teaching and research primarily on gender issues in family and work. Over the past several years, Warner has conducted research on women in nontraditional occupations and gender and family issues. Her most recent article, "Does the Sex of Your Children Matter?" appeared in the Journal of Marriage and the Family, *in November, 1991.*

LOIS B. DeFLEUR, fifth president of the State University of New York at Binghamton, is an eminent sociologist and an experienced administrator. She is the first woman to serve as president of a doctoral degree-granting institution within the New York State University system. Dr. DeFleur is the author of a standard college sociology textbook, now in its fourth edition, and has published widely in scholarly journals. She also served as Provost at the University of Missouri-Columbia and Dean of Humanities and Social Science at Washington State University. She received her B.A. from Blackburn College, M.A. from Indiana University, and Ph.D. from the University of Illinois.

universities increased in the late 1980s following a period of slow growth earlier in the decade. According to this survey, women currently make up 11 percent of presidents of the approximately 3,000 accredited higher education institutions.[1]

It should not be surprising, however, that over half of the women holding academic dean positions are in nursing, home economics, arts and sciences, and continuing education. Within four-year institutions, the largest number of women are employed at liberal arts institutions while male administrators are found more often in comprehensive colleges and universities. According to ACE, women presidents are much more likely to be found at two-year schools. While there has been an increase in women's appointments as CEOs in the last five years, the increase is still most evident in community college settings as compared to large, comprehensive institutions.[2]

What can explain this sex segregation in higher education administration? Sex segregation is not unique to institutions of higher education, but is pervasive throughout the labor market. Explanations for sex segregation are usually divided into two camps: those focusing on characteristics employees bring with them to the labor market (supply side approach), and those which place emphasis on employer characteristics and labor market structure (demand side approach). Sociologists and economists have found empirical support for both perspectives.[3]

The role of personal characteristics in explaining sex segregation and earnings differences has been well researched by sociologists and economists, and is often referred to as "human capital theory" or the supply side approach.[4] From this perspective, individuals are seen as bringing to the labor market a supply of resources which are relatively valuable to employers. Those holding the more desirable resources are more successful in obtaining the higher paying, more prestigious jobs. Women often are disadvantaged in the labor market primarily because they are less likely than men to hold the valued resource of continuous employment records. Because women take time out of the labor market (whether by choice or cultural mandate) they receive less on-the-job training and their previously accumulated skills depreciate in value as they become rusty without use.

As a "profession," administrative careers in higher education are very demanding with respect to required resources. Not only continuous employment, but also advanced education and the willingness to relocate geographically are very important. Researchers have found that lack of advanced degrees, being married and/or having children, and restrictions on geographic mobility disadvantage women in academia.[5]

One of the more important variables that individuals bring with them to the labor market is education. Most of the research focusing on the effect of education on occupational outcomes has measured this variable in terms of the quantity of education (i.e., years completed). In the area of higher education administration, however, amount of education may not be the most relevant dimension. It is rare to find college or university presidents or provosts without a doctoral level degree. What may be more of an issue is the area of study for the advanced degree. Moore argues that for the very top positions in higher education administration (e.g., president, provost, or vice president of academic affairs), certain areas of educational training are more acceptable than others.[6] Traditionally, most senior administrators have come from one of the liberal arts disciplines. Fields such as English, chemistry and history are usually well represented, but this is not surprising since these are among the largest academic disciplines. Specialized degrees such as higher education administration or business administration, however, are sometimes disparaged as not providing a sufficiently academic background for administrative roles. An examination of degrees awarded over the last several decades reveals that men and women are not receiving bachelors or advanced degrees in the same areas. Within the liberal arts and sciences, women are much more numerous in the arts and humanities. There are also more women in all fields of education with a significant number receiving degrees in higher education administration.[7] These differences in fields of study may work to channel or limit men and women as they seek administrative posts.

Most academic administrators also have significant experience in faculty roles and recent studies of their career paths reveal faculty experience as the principal entry point.[8] Typically, they move through the ranks from assistant to full professor as they accumulate accomplishments in their specialized research and teaching areas. Some faculty are chosen by their colleagues to serve as the department chair which is often regarded as the basic foundation for those who want to move into other administrative posts. It may be difficult for managers from government or industry to understand how such faculty experience provides the needed background for academic administration. Colleges and universities are large, complex institutions requiring significant management and fiscal expertise and faculty members typically do not develop this expertise in the normal course of their activities. However, the academic community does not regard this as a serious drawback. Henry Rosovsky, the former Dean of the College of Arts and Sciences at Harvard University, states the case clearly:

> The technical skills of the executive are trivialities compared with understanding the fundamental nature of the university and this has to come from experience acquired by long hours in the library, laboratory, and with students.[9]

We would expect then to find that men and women who have had faculty experience, and especially as chair of a department, to be at an advantage when it comes to obtaining administrative positions.

In sum, the supply side approach to explaining sex segregation in higher education administration would focus on the usual set of human capital factors (amount of education, training, and years of experience), but would also include occupationally specific factors such as the educational area of one's advanced degree and the existence of certain academic experiences such as holding a faculty position.

Increasingly, however, sociologists have been looking at the demand-side approach, or the impact of the organizational structure within which people work on the segregation of women and men in the labor market.[10] The focus of this research is on the informal and formal mechanisms within labor markets (internal, external, and occupational) which can keep individuals from entry into such markets, or restrict their movement within them. Of particular interest to our study of educational administrators are the findings with respect to occupational labor markets. These markets are made up of individuals who have received extensive training and/or education resulting in very specialized skills.[11] Although some occupational labor markets exist within firms, many of the markets cross institutions and require a good amount of geographic mobility. Using this description, higher education administration can be viewed as an occupational labor market.

As the research summarized by Roos and Reskin suggests, occupational labor markets contain institutionalized policies or rules that affect mobility.[12] In higher education, the processes of matching candidates with jobs are carried out largely through faculty-based search committees. The composition and operation of these committees has significant impact on who is considered for top positions in colleges and universities. These committees are composed primarily of senior males even though women and minorities are increasingly represented. This means that even though committees try to locate a wide range of candidates, the bottom line often is that they are most concerned with finding a person who fits in with the existing organization. Members of these committees may feel most comfortable with individuals similar to themselves who they believe will be able to fit in with local community groups and important business and political leaders. In order to move more women and minorities into leadership positions, active intervention in the search and screening process may be required. However, it has been found that even when search committees did put forward minority candidates, they were not often supported by the administration. After comparing the opportunities for men and women during the last decade, Tinsley suggests that if we expect underrepresented groups to be recommended by search committees then institutional leaders as well as governing boards must be committed to these goals and must be actively involved in the recruitment process.[13]

Obtaining good positions in occupational labor markets is often dependent on access to the right networks. These networks spread information about different jobs and carry important information about potential candidates. Langlois suggests that men are more likely than women to have personal contacts available to help them in their entry into these positions. Because men and women are most likely to use same-sex job contacts and academic environments are still heavily male-dominated, women may find themselves at a disadvantage as they try to use networks to gain entry into administrative posts.[14]

Because higher education administration is still a relatively small field with many strong networks, mentoring and sponsorship play a particularly important role in the advancement of women. Mentors help proteges understand the rules of the game, they give positive support for accomplishments and provide feedback on performance. Mentoring relationships also should include sponsorship so that the careers of proteges can be more carefully directed. The sponsors may provide advice about the next step in a career and nominate proteges for important positions. The latter action is particularly significant in higher education since the norms of the search process dictate that candidates should have others nominate them for jobs. It is also important for sponsors to ensure that proteges have opportunities to demonstrate their talents in professional assignments. Therefore, they should be on the lookout for ways to help them. There are studies which indicate that women who have good mentors are more successful in their career advancement. This is particularly true of those who have male mentors since they can help women become known in the "old boy network" which is still a significant force in these occupations. The importance of mentors also may vary over the course of an administrative career. Having a sponsor at the point of entry into an administrative career is particularly advantageous because the particular type of entry into a career is crucial in terms of subsequent career development.[15]

Another feature of occupational labor markets is the patterning of career ladders within them. The work of Rosabeth Kanter shows that it is often the case that women enter an internal labor market in jobs that are part of short career ladders, with little opportunity to change directions. A similar situation may exist with respect to higher education administration where top level administrators in colleges and universities have followed relatively strict paths, each focused on particular administrative functions: personnel services, alumni affairs, business, or academic affairs. Some research suggests that women are more likely to enter into administrative career paths that are clustered in the nonacademic areas of student affairs or other university services.[16] These career paths are more likely to be dead-end or to be on ladders which have low ceilings. It is the area of academic affairs that appears to have the most streamlined path to the top of the administrative hierarchy and in which women are less frequently found. Thus, the point of entry into the administrative career is a crucial area for investigation. Does the first job in administration have important ramifications for the subsequent jobs taken, or is there movement across administrative areas? Also, are women more likely to get a different start from men in their career paths?

As we have pointed out, past research suggested areas of importance for exploring the career paths of higher education administration, but these variables have not been widely investigated. Therefore we set out to survey senior academic administrators on their experiences in three general areas: career development, factors perceived as important for career development, and demographic characteristics. For this chapter, we focused on a subset of these variables with respect to their import for holding certain positions in higher education administration. Our primary dependent variable is the level of one's administrative position in higher education. We initially started with 15 categories for the current position, then collapsed them into four levels: (1) president, academic vice president, provost, or chancellor; (2) nonacademic vice presidents (e.g., VP of finance); (3) academic dean; and (4) nonacademic dean.

With respect to professional experience prior to the current position in higher education administration, we focused on the educational background of respondents and whether or not they had faculty experiences prior to their current position. Areas in which respondents received their highest degree include: arts and humanities, social sciences, physical sciences, business, and education. Respondents were said to have had a faculty path in their professional experience if they held a tenure-track faculty position at any time prior to the current position.

The issue of sponsorship at the port of entry was addressed by asking respondents whether they were sponsored (or nominated) for their first administrative position in higher education or whether they applied for the position independently. The first job variable is operationalized as the first administrative job held in an institution of higher education.

FINDINGS

Sample Description

The data for our study consists of 394 administrators at the dean and above level in all types of institutions of higher education. Of these administrators, 319 (81 percent) are male. In terms of age, the female administrators are somewhat younger (46.7) on average than the male administrators (50). And the overwhelming majority of our respondents classify their racial identification as White (84 percent of women, 93 percent of men).

Familial situations differ markedly for men and women. Although the majority of both women and men are currently married (57 percent of women and 90 percent of men), a notable percentage of women have never been married (33 percent compared to only 3 percent of men) and women are also more likely to be divorced than men. Most of those who are married have spouses who also hold professional occupations. However, men are significantly more likely than women to be married to someone who we characterize as working "at home." Male administrators are also significantly more likely to have children (95 percent) than are female administrators (60 percent).

Data on the educational achievements and current administrative positions of our respondents are presented in Table 1. A majority of women (63 percent) and men (66 percent) hold doctoral level degrees. The area in which the highest degree was received, however, differed for the women and men in our sample. The majority of women received their highest degree in education (60 percent) while the men's backgrounds were more varied with 36 percent receiving their highest degree in education, 17 percent in the social sciences, and 11 percent each in the categories of history/philosophy, physical sciences, and business.

The distribution of current administrative positions shows that men are significantly more likely to be at senior level positions than are women. Men are about equally divided between the levels of "dean" and those levels above dean, while the vast majority of women (70.5) are at the dean level, with most of these in nonacademic dean positions. Using the Carnegie Classification System, type of institution does not differ significantly between women and men, with most administrators in our sample at comprehensive universities, liberal arts colleges, and community colleges. Male and female administrators are also found in relatively equal proportions at public and private institutions.

Education Area and Faculty Experience

As we outlined above, researchers have typically separated factors explaining labor market outcomes into those brought to the market and those features which characterize the organization of markets. We identified two characteristics that individuals bring with them to the market that should have special significance to administrators in higher eduction: educational background in terms of the area in which they received their highest degree, and whether or not administrators have ever held faculty positions. Both of these factors are important for positions in higher education administration because they are indicators of professional academic experience. We expect not only that those who have advanced degrees in the arts and sciences and

Table 1

Descriptive Statistics

	Women%	Men%
Gender	19	81
*Marital Status**		
Married	38.4	77.6
Remarried	17.8	12.8
Divorced	9.6	5.8
Widowed	0	1.0
Never Married	34.2	2.9
*Occupation of Spouse**		
Professional/Technical	83	64
Nonprofessional	4	8
At Home	0	28
Retired	5	0
In School	5	0
Other	5	5
Race/Ethnic Identity		
American Indian, Alaskan Native	3	0
Asian	4	1
Black	8	3
Hispanic	1	3
White	84	93
*Percent with Children**	59.2	94.9
Mean Age	46.7	50.0
Educational Level		
Doctorate	63	66
Master's	35	29
Bachelor's	2	5
*Academic Department of Highest Degree**		
Arts, Humanities	9.5	9
History, Philosophy	3	11
Social Science	12	17
Math, Computer Science	1	5
Physical Sciences	9.5	11
Business	5	11
Education	60	36
*Level of Current Position**		
President/Chancellor	7	15.6
Vice President/Provost	12.7	13.7
Vice President (division)	9.9	22.9
Academic Dean	28.2	26.4
Nonacademic Dean	42.5	21.3
Type of Institution		
Research University	8.5	10.9
Doctoral University	7.0	9.9
Comprehensive University	21.1	25.9
Liberal Arts College	38.0	16.4
Community College	38.0	33.8
Other	1.4	3.1
Funding Source of Institution		
Private	48	47.8
Public	52	52.2

*Indicates a gender difference at $< .05$

those with faculty experience to hold higher positions in the administrative hierarchy compared to those not having these characteristics, but we also expect these individuals to be more likely than others to be in the more academic areas of administration (presidents, academic vice presidents, provosts, academic deans).

As can be seen in Table 2, the expected relationships with respect to the area of education and administrative position are supported. Those with degrees in the social and physical sciences are represented at higher rates than those with degrees in other fields at the most senior level positions. Those from the arts and sciences also show higher representation at the academic dean level. Those with degrees in business and education have greater representation in both of the nonacademic areas, with those holding degrees in business having the largest showing in the senior level nonacademic positions.

These analyses include all administrators, regardless of level of education completed. Although the majority in our sample held doctoral level degrees, about one-third did not, and it seems reasonable to see if our observed relationships hold for those with doctorates in particular. An analysis of those having completed doctoral degrees results in essentially the same relationship between educational area and administrative position, however several cells are small enough that statistical tests become problematic. There are very few with doctoral degrees in the business fields (n=5), and very few Ph.D.s in the arts and physical sciences who hold nonacademic positions.

Looking at the relationship between educational area and admin-

Table 2

Level of Administrative Position by Type of Education

Level	Arts	Social Science	Physical Science	Business	Education
President or Provost	8 22.2	32 33.7	20 37.7	7 19.4	39 25.7
Vice President/ Divisions	4 11.1	17 17.9	8 15.1	21 58.3	30 19.7
Academic Dean	15 41.7	27 28.4	20 37.7	2 5.6	32 21.1
Nonacademic Dean	9 25.0	19 20.0	5 9.4	6 16.7	51 33.6
	36	95	53	36	152

Chi-square = 56.3   d.f. = 12   p = .00

istrative position by gender we see that the expected relationship is found for both men and women, but the relationship is not statistically significant for women (Table 3). We have collapsed educational area for these analyses due to the relatively small sample size for women, but have done so in a way suggested by our previous discussion (i.e., we have collapsed all arts and science degrees into one category and combined the more specialized degrees into the other). For both male and female administrators, the relationship between education and position replicates the general relationship found previously, but the relationship is statistically significant only for men. Although women from arts and sciences backgrounds fare slightly better than women from business and education, the observed relationship doesn't come close to reaching significance. Again, we controlled for level of education by observing only those with doctoral level degrees. For men, the relationship is still the same, and significant. For women, the same relationship is observed but the sample size is insufficient for statistical tests.

Turning to the issue of faculty experience, we find that it also shows the predicted relationship to the type of administrative position held regardless of gender. Table 4 shows that administrators with faculty experience are significantly more likely to be in the highest level positions (president and provost) as well as academic dean positions

Table 3

Educational Area and Administrative Position, by Gender

Level	Women		Men	
	Arts & Sciences	Business & Education	Arts & Sciences	Business & Education
President or Provost	6 24.0	9 19.6	54 33.8	37 26.1
Vice President/ Divisions	3 12.0	5 10.9	26 16.3	46 32.4
Academic Dean	7 28.0	11 23.9	56 35.0	23 16.2
Nonacademic Dean	9 36.0	21 45.7	24 15.0	36 25.4
	25	46	160	142

Chi-square = .633
d.f. = 3
P = .89

Chi-square = 23.93
d.f. = 3
p = .00

than are those without faculty experience. Administrators without faculty backgrounds are found more often than those with faculty experience in the nonacademic areas, but men are much more likely than women without faculty experience to make it to the senior level nonacademic positions (vice president of divisions).

It seems especially important here to control for level of education, as the difference between having and not having faculty experience in higher education may be due to having or not having completed doctoral training. An analysis of only those with doctorates, however, shows the same relationship as we found in the entire sample.

Sponsorship and Entry Position

In addition to the characteristics brought to the market, we also identified several features of the educational administration labor market which we believe will have some bearing on the positions held within it. Because of the nature of the profession, we suggested that sponsorship at entry to administrative careers as well as the type of position held early in the career will have an effect on positions attained later. Specifically, we hypothesized that sponsorship will work to an administrator's advantage and enhance movement up the hierarchy. Following the work on internal labor markets, we also expect that the

Table 4

Level of Administrative Position by Career Path, Controlling for Gender

	Women		Men	
	Nonfaculty	Faculty	Nonfaculty	Faculty
President or Provost	7 17.9	9 27.3	30 21.0	64 37.0
Vice President/ Divisions	6 15.4	2 6.1	51 35.7	23 13.3
Academic Dean	3 7.7	15 45.5	24 16.8	59 34.1
Nonacademic Dean	23 69.0	7 21.2	38 26.6	27 15.6
	39	33	143	173

Chi-square = 18.4   Chi-square = 37.0
d.f. = 3   d.f. = 3
P = .00   p = .00

first job held in the administrative career will tend to segregate administrators into academic and nonacademic careers.

Table 5 shows the relationship between sponsorship and administrative position for women and men. For women a significant relationship exists between these two variables. Specifically, women are more likely to be in the academic administrative positions, and more likely to be in the top level positions if they are sponsored at entry rather than if they actively sought their first administrative jobs. It is interesting to note that for men a similar relationship exists, but it is not statistically significant. Male administrators are just as likely to reach senior level positions without sponsorship as they are with sponsorship.

Table 5

Sponsorship and Administrative Position, by Gender

| Level | Women | | Men | |
	Actively Sought	Recruited	Actively Sought	Recruited
President or Provost	4 14.8	10 25.0	37 28.7	54 31.4
Vice President/ Divisions	5 18.5	3 7.5	33 25.6	37 21.5
Academic Dean	3 11.1	14 35.0	32 24.8	48 27.9
Nonacademic Dean	15 55.6	13 32.5	27 20.9	33 19.2
	27	40	129	172

Women: Chi-square = 8.11, d.f. = 3, P = .04

Men: Chi-square = 1.08, d.f. = 3, p = .78

Looking at Table 6, we find that our predictions with respect to the relationship between first and current positions in administration also are supported. For these analyses we have eliminated those who have only held one administrative position, focusing on those who have changed positions at least once. In addition, it was necessary to collapse categories, given that very few administrators started their careers as presidents, provosts or academic vice presidents. We have created four categories: (1) senior academic positions (dean and above); (2) senior nonacademic (dean and above); (3) junior academic (academic positions

Table 6

Relationship Between First Job Held and Current Position

Level	Senior Academic	Senior Nonacademic	Junior Academic	Junior Nonacademic
President or Provost	30 50.8	14 25.0	18 30.0	36 27.3
Vice President/ Divisions	5 8.5	19 33.9	8 13.3	38 28.8
Academic Dean	23 39.0	4 7.1	27 45.0	25 18.9
Nonacademic Dean	1 1.7	19 33.9	7 11.7	33 25.0
	59	56	60	132

Chi-square = 63.24   d.f. = 9   p = .00

below dean such as assistant dean or chair of an academic department); and (4) junior nonacademic (nonacademic below dean such as directors or registrars). The data in Table 6 suggest that although there is some degree of movement across areas of higher education, there are primarily two tracks: academic and nonacademic paths. Specifically, we find that those who begin their administrative career in the academic areas are significantly more likely than those starting in nonacademic positions to attain the most senior level position of president and the highest academic position of provost, or academic vice president. Those starting in nonacademic administrative positions are considerably more likely to attain a nonacademic divisional vice presidency.

An important question arises following our findings whether educational background and the start in a career affect subsequent administrative positions (i.e., are both independently related to administrative career attainments?). Perhaps the educational background channels individuals into certain areas and then the paths are set. In Table 7 we look at the effect of starting position controlling for area of education. We find that regardless of educational background, the beginning position in administration has a significant effect on current positions held. Whether the degree is in arts and sciences or in business or educational fields, those who start their administrative careers in academic areas are more likely subsequently to attain senior level positions.

Table 7

Relationship Between First Job and Current Administrative Position Controlling for Area of Advanced Degree

Level	Arts & Sciences		Education & Business	
	Academic	Nonacademic	Academic	Nonacademic
President or Provost	37 / 43.0	14 / 24.1	10 / 33.3	33 / 27.0
Vice President/ Divisions	9 / 10.5	16 / 27.6	4 / 13.3	40 / 32.8
Academic Dean	38 / 44.2	10 / 17.2	11 / 36.7	17 / 13.9
Nonacademic Dean	2 / 2.3	18 / 31.0	5 / 16.7	32 / 26.2
	86	58	30	122

Chi-square = 37.4
d.f. = 3
P = .00

Chi-square = 11.1
d.f. = 3
p = .01

DISCUSSION AND CONCLUSIONS

We began this chapter by examining some of the reasons behind the occupational segregation in higher education administration that has been documented in the literature. Specifically, we wanted to explore why women are not as likely to attain the top administrative positions in colleges and universities, and why they are more likely to be found in nonacademic administrative posts than are men. Using the perspectives developed in sociological and economic literature, we identified several factors that should be relevant for career attainment in higher education administration. These included education and faculty experience as well as the occupational market factors of sponsorship and the entry position.

Our research suggests that both supply and demand factors are important in higher education administration, although all of them are not equally important for men and women. We find, for example, that the educational degree area affects current administrative positions, but it is more important for men than women. Although degrees in the arts and sciences increase the likelihood of holding academic administrative positions, only the results for men are statistically significant. In addition, having a sponsor is significantly related to current positions only for women. Women fare better when they are sponsored, but this is not the case for men. These findings suggest that careers in higher education administration may be more restrictive for women than for men.

The effect of other variables on administrative positions did not show a gender difference. For example, the effect of faculty experience is significantly related to holding senior positions for both men and women. Not surprisingly, men are more likely to reach more senior positions within both academic and nonacademic areas.

Although our findings demonstrate the importance of factors typically categorized as "supply" and "demand" side factors, some theoretical caution is necessary. England et al. argues very convincingly that supply characteristics are often described as a function of personal choice (i.e., individuals accumulate experiences that they select and this takes place outside the market model).[17] However, women may not easily be able to control their choices. Labor market conditions and cultural pressures may channel women into certain types of educational fields and thus impact their likelihood of obtaining faculty and administrative positions. Women also may be at a disadvantage because of subtle variables that come into play as they compete for leadership positions. We have already mentioned the impact of search committees in the selection process and an important part of the assessment is a determination of the leadership capabilities of candidates. Women must deal with the stereotypes associated with conceptions of leadership in American society. Traditionally, the qualities and behaviors expected of leaders are those associated with masculinity—aggressiveness, independence, authority, and confidence. Thus it may be more difficult for people to see these qualities in women. It has been reported that women have not been selected for senior positions because they may not "look" or "act like" a dean, vice president, or president. Changing these perceptions so that women are more readily accepted in leadership roles will take many years.

Another factor that may impact the selection of administrators is the ability to meet social expectations. Administrators represent their schools in a variety of community and professional groups and they are expected to host a large number of social events. Some people assume that these activities should be carried out with the traditional husband and wife team. This may pose problems for women administrators since only about one-half of them are currently married.[18] In contrast, almost all (90 percent) male administrators are married and fewer than half of their wives have full-time employment, so it is possible for them to be supportive in meeting the social demands of these roles.

Another consideration is whether women actually aspire to higher education administrative roles and want to move through the requisite career paths. One of the questions in our survey asks about the occupational goals of respondents, and we find that women are slightly more likely than their male counterparts to seek promotion. Thus, women have the aspirations even though it may not be as easy for them to seek these roles because of their family characteristics. Men typically experience several geographical moves during their careers but patterns for women administrators are different.[19] Women are not as mobile as men and one reason is because many women administrators have spouses who are also pursuing careers. Also some women under consideration for senior positions may not have followed a typical career path several decades ago because they had difficulty finding regular academic employment. Others may have interrupted their careers to accommodate child rearing and thus may not be as far along professionally as their male colleagues. We find particularly that many women have not had experience as department chairs which may hinder them as they try to move into other administrative roles.

In sum, our data support the notion of identifiable career tracks within the occupational labor market of higher education administration. Our data also suggest that career paths in higher education are structured differently for men and women. Women are disproportionately represented in the lower levels of administrative positions and many are in nonacademic tracks even though they have similar educational experiences as men. It appears, then, that if women are to advance to senior posts in higher education that some intervention strategies may be needed. In the last decade or so several professional organizations have designed programs specifically to help women move into leadership roles. Examples of these programs are the Summer Institute for Women in Higher Education Administration at Bryn Mawr College, and the American Council on Education's National Identification Program.[20] The goals of these programs are to enhance the skills of individual women as well as to address some factors in the search processes and the institutions themselves that may pose barriers to the advancement of women. As we continue to monitor the career paths of women and men in educational administration, the impact of such programs will continue to be assessed.

ABSTRACT

Trained from Pee Wee League football or baseball onward—team-work is a natural for men, but women, at least until very recently, often find themselves at a loss in the managerial milieu. While most men already know certain basic "ground rules" of institutional life, many women have to learn about organizational dynamics the hard way—through experience. This chapter provides observations and anecdotes for women who aspire to executive level management positions in higher education. It is the author's contention that if women can learn more about the dynamics of organizational culture while at the same time retaining their traditional nurturing role, they will inevitably move into more influential roles on campus.

Chapter Two

Women, Leadership, and the Academy:
Anecdotes and Observations

Carol C. Harter

As the title of this chapter suggests, I came to this subject not as a scholar or researcher on the subject of women in the academy: I just are one. And while my natural curiosity leads me to read just about every article or study that attempts in some way to grapple with the fate of women in higher education—everything from statistical and descriptive surveys to less quantitative analyses that explore the climate for women on campuses—the major source of my remarks is my own experience both as a faculty member and administrator for over 20 years.

My career exemplifies the nontraditional pattern that characterizes the careers of most women administrators in my, or earlier, genera-

CAROL C. HARTER *is the eleventh and first woman President of the State University of New York at Geneseo, a position she has held since July 1989. Geneseo enrolls 5,000 students, employs over 800 staff and faculty, and has total operating budgets of approximately $60 million. Prior to being named president, Dr. Harter served as vice president for administration at Ohio University. A native of New York City, she earned her B.A., M.A., and Ph.D. degrees in English and American Literature at SUNY-Binghamton, and an honorary doctor of Humane Letters degree from Ohio University. She also earned a certificate from the Institute for Educational Management at Harvard University.*

tions—from English faculty member to Ombudsman to Vice President and Dean of Students to Vice President for Administration—illustrative of the classic nontraditional career. And, admittedly, these moves were much more likely within a single institution than they would have been had I sought such opportunities on several different campuses. The key for me has been a willingness to sacrifice for some considerable time the opportunity to move elsewhere in order to capitalize on the potential for career growth at my own institution; this internal movement is also characteristic of many women, including women presidents, and often represents a strategic approach to career growth. In any case, moving from chief student affairs officer to chief administrative officer would have been highly unlikely had I been seeking such a change at another university. The opportunity to assume responsibility rarely associated with a woman, much less a Faulkner scholar, has, however, proved extraordinarily fruitful in many ways—for both my own professional growth and, I hope, for the well-being of the university.

But being a seasoned professional has come through the school of hard knocks, and I am an honors graduate of that school. During the course of my career development, I have learned a number of things through painful experience and by trial and error which men already seem to know but women frequently do not. I think women do not always acquire this learning for at least two reasons: (1) our training and acculturation is different from men's; and (2) our unusual career patterns sometimes thrust us into difficult and visible roles before we have accumulated the experiential learning which is so often characteristic of our male counterparts.

While most men (and the few women who might have traditional administrative experience) already know certain basic "ground rules" of institutional life, I had to learn the following about organizational dynamics: (1) teamwork and all it implies is the key to effective management; (2) commitment and loyalty to the organization and its goals must supersede personal ego and personal reward; (3) an executive level administrator or manager is a generalist, not a specialist or a technician (in fact, the higher one rises in the organization, the closer one gets to being the "least productive" person in it, but paradoxically, the most important); and, (4) individual achievement as a manager is directly tied to institutional progress and success and cannot exist apart from the larger context of the organization.

I call attention to these almost embarrassingly obvious discoveries because they represent not always understood, but critical lessons that one fails to learn at one's peril. Moreover, my own experience supervising others, particularly women staff, has reinforced my sense of the importance of these lessons. I have been most fortunate, for example, to have been both a mentor and boss to a number of extraordinarily talented women who have gone on to increasingly responsible careers in higher education both at my own institution and elsewhere; indeed, I have found the mentoring of other women, where I can do it effectively, one of the greatest rewards of administrative work. What I found difficult—and frankly unexpected—were the two cases of failure I experienced dealing with bright women who could not or would not learn some of these basic lessons; as a result, they sought—and were encouraged to seek—work outside higher education and outside traditional organizational structures. Both of these women had values at odds with the so-called organizational culture; in fact, both had attitudes that are more common to higher education settings than to other types of organizations and are frequently typical of faculty members, particularly women faculty aspiring to administrative roles or careers.

It is common wisdom in higher education that an inherent distrust often exists between faculty and administrators and that, probably at best, a fragile—and one hopes, a creative—detente can be achieved. I believe the basis of this inevitable tension arises from the individualistic nature and impulses of faculty in conflict with the communal nature of administrative work. That is, faculty are trained to be individual thinkers, critics, researchers, scholars, and artists, and attempt in their teaching to engender those values in students. As good faculty, we want our students to become thoughtful and responsible individuals.

As administrators, however, our jobs are attuned to the well-being of the community as a whole: to the greatest good for the greatest number. Our thrust is therefore different from the faculty's and must, by definition, stress communal values—holistic planning, the future health of the entire university or college—group processes and activities aimed at serving a multiplicity of complex needs. This tension between the individual and the communal is, I believe, at the root of some of the conflict between administrative and faculty goals and the processes of perception, and must be tolerated and held in a delicate balance by the best of both groups. The inherent difference in values between the two groups is, in my experience, exaggerated in some women, particularly faculty, because we pride ourselves in individual achievement, and individual recognition.

When one seeks a leadership role on campus, however, one must sublimate some of this reliance on individuality; in fact, individual needs become subordinate to the well-being of the community we are asked to serve in a university setting. Ego must be sublimated; rewards will be indirect; praise will be rare.

I found this shift from the individually oriented to the community-centered most disconcerting: I missed the direct reward of influencing a student's growth by seeing his or her eyes light up with intellectual or aesthetic insight; the time simply to think; the satisfaction of publishing an article and experiencing the collegial recognition that flows from that activity; the freedom to organize most of my professional time to suit my own needs. But these discrete, often highly personal, experiences largely disappear in the administrative world and I continue to create opportunities to reintroduce them into my life whenever possible. But one must adjust to the shift in emphasis and to its significance quickly if one wishes to develop into an effective leader in higher education. It is the job of administration to serve others—to create and nurture the environment that allows faculty to grow as individual teachers and researchers and to stimulate similar growth in students. And, paradoxically, it takes community-oriented leaders to make the fullest individual development possible.

The two young women I spoke of earlier were unable to grasp that essential paradox—they found it impossible to sublimate their egos; they were unable to work effectively with others in team relationships because they used confrontation as their primary mode of communication; they were unable to transcend their need for constant personal praise and reinforcement; they refused to place their work or opinions in the largest institutional context—they could not see how every decision limits or affects every other decision. They failed to understand that rewards can be indirect and that the measure of a successful leader is ultimately the realization of the organization's goals. They also failed to recognize, as many women do, that institutional politics can be subtly influenced, but can neither be ignored nor radically altered.

Now this is not to say that many men are not guilty of these same failures to perceive the demands and measures of leadership. As we all know, the history of failures in leadership is writ large with the names of hubristic men. My point is that women, because of their traditional acculturation, are less likely to come to leadership roles in higher education with well-developed skills and sophisticated organizational experiences and are therefore more vulnerable to making naive mistakes in failing to understand the nature of administrative work.

I suspect for most men—trained from Pee Wee League football or baseball onward—teamwork is natural, attention to team goals is obvious. But for women—at least until very recently—individual athletic performance, personal accomplishment, technical or specialized skill development were (and still often are) the culturally accepted and reinforced values women were taught. These values are not in and of themselves negative ones; but they work against women's adjustment to the organizational setting and managerial or administrative success. Taught early to be simultaneously competitive and team supportive, men usually find management a natural extension of the boyhood world and their already carefully learned experience. Women, however (myself included at an early stage), products of a different environment and different expectations, find themselves at a loss to understand and integrate themselves easily into the managerial milieu.

In addition to this generalized learning about the nature of organizational and team values, the most important learning I acquired in the early stages of my administrative career was stylistic as opposed to substantive. (I acquired substantive knowledge pretty much on my own.) Indeed, most of this stylistic knowledge was passed on, often unconsciously, by male executives; I watched and learned from people who were supportive of my career development and who were themselves not only successful, but humane and progressive administrators. I learned to observe them carefully and to analyze consciously what characteristics they seemed to possess in common, regardless of idiosyncrasies of style, personality, or the unique local conditions in which they carried out their work. As a result of these observations and my own subsequent experience, there are several generalizations I would make for all those who aspire to executive level management positions in higher education, particularly women.

Outstanding educational leaders share:

1. A belief that strong leadership can make a difference—they are self-aware, people-oriented, tone-setters;
2. An institutional perspective and an inclination to see the larger whole—they are holistic thinkers;
3. A devotion to teamwork and to achieving, by various strategies, consensus in decision-making—they are team leaders;
4. A demonstrated record of sound management practice, whether through direct leadership or through delegation to superior management staff—they are good administrators;
5. Highly developed and sophisticated public relations and communications skills (the ability to analyze, synthesize, and articulate)—they are effective public presences in person and in print;
6. Extraordinarily accurate political awareness and insight into current and potential issues which affect higher education—they are skilled politicians;
7. Remarkable good health, personal charisma, energy, a high tolerance for ambiguity, and a saving sense of humor—they are magnetic human beings.

While these are characteristics shared by many successful professionals, whether they be male or female, some of these characteristics are, I believe, more difficult to acquire for women than for men.

1. Women need to gain self-confidence and understand that they can self-consciously establish a leadership tone just as men so naturally do. They can also indulge their people orientation—no matter how many material resources you must push around and account for, the people one serves, works with, and works for are the beginning and end of managing;

2. Women need to learn that perfection at individual tasks or details means virtually nothing—the translation of focused activity to broad issues or problems is the key to developing an executive perspective;

3. Women need to understand the ground rules and dynamics of teamwork to which most males come already, sometimes unconsciously, prepared; women need to learn that administrative work involves constant, on-going planning and negotiation. Forever dealing with crisis management and/or retreating to unalterable declarations of principle (when a little compromise will get the task accomplished and save everyone's face) will inevitably lead to powerlessness;

4. Women need to embrace the responsibilities of leadership and establish management credibility rapidly; the nurturing, supportive training of women needs to be blended with (not sacrificed for) the no-nonsense, traditional assertiveness of male counterparts; competency at traditional male activities (budgeting, labor relations, finance, legislative liaison) needs to be demonstrated; the syndrome of "math anxiety" women suffer, and its analogues in higher education administration, must be confronted and overcome by additional formal training if necessary.

5. Women need to learn (and so do men) that an effective public presence does not require a 6 foot 5 inch frame and a basso profundo voice; while some people, mostly men, have a clear advantage by the sheer ability to be physically intimidating and impressive, others can overcome their implicit "liabilities" by preparing thoroughly for ceremonial and public occasions, communicating effectively and, if they are women, enjoying and being comfortable as women at the same time they refuse to use their sexuality in stereotypically feminine ways;

6. Women need to learn to become "political" and simultaneously retain their integrity—the two are not mutually exclusive. While we do not always have access to the typical networking which goes on at golf courses, in locker rooms, or over urinals, we need to learn how to enter some of these alien arenas and to invite others into the networking arenas in which we are most comfortable. Being "one of the boys" can cause problems, but learning how to read the political landscape and where the real power is can only be accomplished with some entree into the arenas occupied by successful and influential men;

7. While no one can create a healthy body out of an unhealthy one, I have discovered that the good health of executives is no simple biological phenomenon of the survival of the fittest. Much good health is self-willed and represents a determination

not to succumb to petty physical annoyances; taking care of oneself is the obligation of executives and the result is an image of a kind of invulnerability—of a kind of toughness that is associated with success and the ability to bear a great many burdens without collapsing. Ambitious women need to be realistic and recognize this reality at the same time they protect themselves from real jeopardy to their physical well-being—knowing the difference is the test.

Women also need to enjoy their womanhood, and for heaven's sake, to take themselves less seriously. If there is one characteristic which repeatedly reappears in my observations of ambitious women, it is the lack of a genuine sense of humor—if not the lack thereof, then the repression of whatever sense of humor they might otherwise indulge. The threat, of course, is that we won't be taken seriously or that the stereotypical "silly broad" image will eradicate other accomplishments so painfully gained. Whoever said success and utter seriousness are synonymous? Knowing when to be serious and when to indulge your sense of humor is the only legitimate question; the best administrator I know has an almost uncanny ability to use humor for the purposes of achieving administrative goals and of humanizing the most intense situations.

Women particularly need to learn to relax, to feel comfortable being themselves, to indulge their wit, to display personal individuality and charm, and to be grateful for their energy. And by the way, to recognize, if they make it, that luck and timing were right—no one enters the executive world purely on talent and merit. And last, women need to teach the things they learn and experience to other women by being role models and mentors. It is necessary to be no-nonsense tough on women with whom one works or supervises when they make mistakes; it is imperative, however, to support and nourish their growth when they show real promise; they will be grateful for having the female mentor most of us never had.

If women can learn more about the dynamics of organizational culture—a culture which, after all, was created, nourished, defined, and sustained by men—at the same time they retain the nurturing values of traditional femininity, they will inevitably move into the most influential roles. And higher education, our students, and our colleagues will be the beneficiaries.

ABSTRACT

One of the questions I am asked often is how do you get started on the path to advancement? What are the first steps? How do you get the attention of those who could help you advance? I have a short series of responses for these questions; however the larger question is "How can I advance when the traditional options do not work for me?" The short answers to the first question are: become highly competent in your assignment, show initiative in solving problems, and demonstrate ability to work effectively as an individual and in a group.

But how can you advance when you use these traditional methods and they don't work for you? Women and minorities often find themselves facing this situation. The goal of this chapter is to examine alternative strategies for advancement in the academic environment when traditional paths to advancement appear to be closed. Examples cited are in the community college environment in California.

Chapter Three

Non-traditional Paths to Advancement:
The California Community College Experience

Del M. Anderson

*C*alifornia community college women have advanced to management positions in significant numbers during the last ten years. The reasons are two-fold. First, community college missions encompass both traditional academic curricula and vocational education as well as supportive student services and community services. They have a greater percentage of minority students and adult learners. As a result, this environment has produced a much more egalitarian ethic than can be found in four-year colleges and universities.

Second, women in the community colleges in California have shown greater organizational effectiveness in creating a network to position themselves for advancement while simultaneously confronting traditional male and institutional behaviors. For example, the first annual "Women's Leadership Network" was organized in 1984 to prepare women for leadership roles at the administrative, faculty, and classified support staff levels in the community college.

In 1988, the first annual Hispanic Women in California Community Colleges Leadership Conference was held at Southwestern College in Chula Vista, California (near San Diego). This organization later received funding from the Chancellor's Office of the California Com-

DEL M. ANDERSON is the President of San Jose City College in San Jose, California. President Anderson has been a community college administrator for 15 years. She received her B.A. in Child Development and M.S.W. from San Diego State University and has held positions as vice-president of instruction at Skyline College, Dean of Students at Los Angeles Harbor College, and Dean of Guidance Services at Grossmont College.

munity Colleges. It has become known as the Latina Leadership Network and has annual regional conferences and a state-wide conference that draws nearly 500 people. In 1989, the California Community Colleges Black Women's Leadership Network was organized and is now an annual state-wide, three-day conference that is attended by 200-300 African-American women each year.

Many dynamic women were active and/or held membership in all three networks. Women not only helped each other, they confronted traditional male behaviors both personally and in institutional contexts with sensitivity and determination. They requested and received institutional funding to assist in the support needed to sustain these efforts. The visible support of men is apparent in each network.

At this writing, of the 107 community colleges in California, 28 (or 26 percent) are headed by a woman president or chief executive officer. Of the 28, four are African-American, one is Hispanic, and one is Asian. Thirty-eight percent of the chief instructional officers are women and 26 percent of the chief student services officers are women.

Data at the entry and mid-management levels are more difficult to document. Data in the *Directory of California Colleges* show there are 678 positions with the title of dean, associate dean, or assistant dean. Of the 678 positions, 249 (or 37 percent) are held by women. Of 429 publicly elected trustees, 141 (or 33 percent) are women. Of 107 presidents of academic senates, 38 (or 36 percent) are women. A decade of sustained effort has yielded substantial numbers of women "in the pipeline" and ready for advancement to the next level.

TYPICAL PATHS OF ADVANCEMENT

The typical path for advancing from entry level to the executive level in California Community Colleges is through the academic ranks. Typically a faculty member is elected by peers to serve as chair of an academic discipline or cluster of related disciplines. While some chair positions are management level, increasingly they are members of the collective bargaining unit. Either way, service as chair is the traditional first step to advancement to management.

There are several advantages to serving in an elected chair position. First, it confers academic legitimacy that makes it easier to be identified and accepted as "a leader." Second, it makes for a more orderly transition when contrasted with candidates who use non-traditional routes to advancement. For whatever reasons, women and people of color traditionally have had greater difficulty getting elected as chairs of an academic discipline. There seems to be an invisible gatekeeper at both the discipline chair position and the chief academic officer position that has resulted in these positions being "reserved" for white males and it has been the exceptional female or person of color who could transcend this unidentified gate. Therefore, it is critical that women deliberately target these positions and develop the skills and attributes necessary to succeed.

Academic Senate Leadership

While the transition from a faculty position to election as a chair is the traditional path to advancement to the entry level of management, the second most common option is the move from President of the Academic Senate.

Many institutions identify the role of Academic Senate President as a critical leadership position. Recent legislative changes in California strengthening shared governance, also enhance the opportunity for faculty leadership in institutional matters. An Academic Senate President who demonstrates she not only will represent a constituency, but also can understand institutional perspectives, can frequently bypass the elected chair experience. Academic Senate Presidents become players on a larger stage involving high level decision-making encounters with chief executive officers such as presidents, chancellors, and board members. Many Academic Senate Presidents gain a broader perspective of issues by serving as officers in the state-wide Academic Senate where they interact with and have the opportunity to influence legislators, members of the California Post-Secondary Education Commission, the Chancellor of the California Community Colleges, and other key decision-makers.

The Academic Senate as a path to advancement is not without its pitfalls, however. Senate leaders who advance to management sometimes suffer ridicule at the hands of their former constituents who determine that all of their moves were designed for their own advancement. New management colleagues watch for signs that loyalties will be with faculty when there are issues generating conflict between administrators and faculty. Loss of credibility and charges of hypocrisy are often part of the transition. Faculty who travel this route find there can be difficulty making the transition from leadership by consensus inherent in ascribed authority of a management position. Maintaining credibility with former faculty colleagues and new management colleagues is one of the major developmental tasks for the faculty who make this transition.

Union Leadership

The path from chief union negotiator is another, although infrequent, faculty leadership path used for advancement to the first level of management. Typically, this path is defined with much animosity and charges of "selling-out" on the part of faculty members and "co-optation" by management. Earning credibility can be very difficult under these circumstances.

The Trusted Assistant

In some highly centralized systems, the executive assistant to the chief executive officer will be named to a position such as dean, vice president, or president. While the assistant may have served in a faculty leadership role, more typically, the appointment involves a trusted assistant who has accompanied the chief executive officer on one or more assignments. Those who travel this path enjoy the support of the CEO, but lack the credibility earned by advancing through the ranks and often suffer the derision associated with political cronyism.

Experiences Across Divisions

Another path to advancement is achieved by gaining experience in more than one of the major divisions of the college. California Community Colleges typically have three major organizational divisions: instruction, student services and business, maintenance and operations. Typically, instructional personnel consist of teaching faculty, librarians, instructional aides, and sometimes counselors. More frequently, counselors are part of student services where they serve in traditional counseling programs and along with counselors and support staff in other programs such as Extended Opportunities, Disabled Students, Admissions and Records, Student Activities, and Health Services.

Counselors and other student services personnel who meet minimum qualifications for teaching in an academic discipline such as psychology may find they have an opportunity for advancement through one of the academic divisions of the college. This path is made easier if they have demonstrated leadership in areas such as the Academic Senate, curriculum committee, articulation with colleges and universities, or other areas significant to the college.

Appointment from Outside the College

Increasingly the first level of management is filled through a competitive process where a faculty member in a coordinating or quasi-administrative role from one college competes for an entry level management position on another campus. This results from affirmative action requirements that opportunities for advancement be opened up to a wide variety of potential applicants. So, a faculty member, leader, or program coordinator will compete for an entry level management position at another college. Competitors using this path have a distinct advantage because it is difficult to discern the true nature of their strengths and weaknesses from a distance. Competitors who are native to their college are generally well known by those evaluating them; any weaknesses they have will, therefore, be much harder to conceal than a competitor from another college.

OPTIONS FOR ADVANCEMENT TO MID-MANAGEMENT

Once the first level of management has been attained, by whatever means, there are still paths that are prescribed by tradition where knowledge and understanding of non-traditional options are useful for further advancement. The mid-management positions are typically dean or vice president of a division of the college. Generally, academic deans advance to chief academic officers and student services practitioners advance to chief student services officers.

While first-level and mid-managers must spend a certain amount of time gaining technical competence in their assigned roles, they now have broad fiscal and institutional responsibilities. While they still have well-defined constituencies, they are also responsible for the institution as a whole. Their decisions carry weight beyond the bounds of their primary responsibility; they are part of the "leadership team." It can take three to five years for a person to gain mastery of the technical, divisional, and institutional responsibilities associated with mid-management positions.

While mid-managers could gain valuable experience serving in two or more divisions of the college, breadth is difficult to obtain because of the time constraints described above and because tradition prescribes advancement through depth rather than breadth. At higher levels of management, breadth of experience is a very useful attribute because it conveys greater understanding of the institution as a whole.

First-level and mid-managers can make a conscious effort to gain experience in other divisions of the college without making an actual transfer by serving on committees in other divisions and taking on responsibilities for programs or services that cross divisional boundaries. For student services personnel, service on the Academic Senate, as transfer and/or matriculation officer, membership on the curriculum committee, chair of accreditation self-study committees, membership on the accreditation team of another college, or membership on budget and planning committees can broaden the traditional student services assignment.

Tradition can be a formidable barrier to gaining experience outside of one's area of assignment, therefore, opportunities should be taken when they present themselves. Academic administrators only need sufficient experience to demonstrate mastery of an academic division and the broader institutional perspective. Student services and budget personnel must demonstrate competence in their own areas, but should make a conscious effort to gain academic experience and good supervisory skills to enhance their opportunities for advancement.

FROM MID-MANAGEMENT TO SENIOR MANAGEMENT

After the mid-level of management, the traditional path to senior management is from academic dean of a division to chief academic officer (typically vice president for instruction). It is unusual for the chief academic officer to be appointed from any division outside of the academic divisions. In some colleges, the chief academic officer and chief student services officer are combined in one vice president position. Anyone opting for this path should begin with the understanding that managing both the academic and student services functions will be sufficiently challenging and that they should not plan to remain in such an assignment for more than three years, after which time they should be looking for a position of chief instructional officer or president.

FROM SENIOR MANAGEMENT TO COLLEGE PRESIDENT

College presidents are typically chosen from among the ranks of the chief academic officers, who are responsible, among other things, for oversight of the curriculum and faculty development. The chief student services officer is responsible for instructional support and student matriculation and development. The chief business/operations officer is responsible for the budget, plant maintenance and operations. Any one of these executives can advance to the position of president; however, the path from chief academic officer to president is the traditional path. At this writing, it is estimated that 70 community college presidents in California previously served as chief instructional officer, 24 as chief student services officer, and three as chief business officer. The following is a look at the non-traditional path of these senior management positions to the position of president.

Chief Student Services Officer to President

Since the center of the educational enterprise is classroom teaching, it is rare that a president without teaching experience will be selected. However, chief student services officers constitute the most significant number of non-traditional appointments to president. In the California Community Colleges, 24 presidents are known to have served as counselor/student professional and/or chief student services officer early in their careers.

Student services professionals will have a better chance for advancement to president if they have achieved one or more of the following: a master's degree or credential in an academic discipline, instructional experience in the classroom, and service as chair of an academic discipline.

Chief Business Officer to President

The chief business officer is responsible for overall development and monitoring of the institution's budget. Frequently this position also supervises the physical plant, maintenance, and operations functions. Advancement from chief business officer to president occurs less frequently and is more likely under conditions where there have been fiscal problems. Chief business officers who would advance to president must make a conscious effort to develop and maintain excellent human relations and supervisory skills. They must also demonstrate that they understand not only the fiscal needs of the institution but also the teaching and learning needs of faculty and students.

Advancement to president from community education and other positions outside of higher education do occur but not in sufficient numbers to be included here.

STRATEGIES FOR ADVANCEMENT

When using non-traditional options for advancement, it is important to have gained credible experience at the center of the institution through classroom teaching, service on curriculum committees, and involvement in issues of current concern such as community college transfers, articulation with four-year colleges and universities, and grant-writing, among others. These areas provide opportunities for leadership beyond one's immediate area of assignment.

Many opportunities for leadership arise for people with problem-solving skills, including special, temporary, and "clean-up" assignments, assignments involving more than one function, and highly challenging assignments.

The importance of scholarship should not be underestimated. Scholarship involves more than research and publication—it involves continuing study in one's field or area of assignment and is a prerequisite to maintaining credibility in a teaching and learning environment.

Issues related specifically to the woman as leader need to be understood and addressed. The question of toughness—as in "will she be tough enough?"—is a barrier facing many women who must strike an acceptable balance between assertiveness and aggressiveness. There is a changing pattern in women's leadership styles. Historically, women who have made it in a man's world did so by emulating men's leadership styles. Management styles of both men and women are changing to incorporate a more "androgynous" management style. More will be said about this in Chapter Five.

Women leaders do not have the same personal support system that men have. While wives are expected to assist their husbands who are presidents, no such expectation exists for women presidents. Be aware of stereotypes about women; but don't be consumed by or give too much attention to them. Fight effectively; don't whine or complain without a plan of action. Accept the fact that women leaders are under more and qualitatively different scrutiny than their male counterparts.

Women should choose their bosses carefully because a supervisor sets the outer limits of what they can do or be in the work environment. Learn as much about the boss as the boss knows about you. Talk to people your boss has supervised to find out what he or she was like as a supervisor and what can be expected in the way of mentoring and commitment to the development of staff. It is equally important to determine the goodness of fit between yourself and the institution and staff before accepting a new assignment.

Women should take advantage of any opportunities to gain depth in their current assignments while also gaining breadth through experience in related areas that are institution-wide and not limited to any one division of the college.

ABSTRACT

Statistics measuring the overall status of women in higher education have shown without question that the profile of women's positions and the progression of their careers vary significantly from the male norm.

In fact, we now have a situation in which two sets of norms coexist. On the one hand, we have new social and political commitments to individual equality, openness of opportunity, and equal responsibility for men and women, and, on the other, old beliefs in the fact and rightness of inequality—in the fact and rightness of a distinction between men and women in their capacities and proper roles. We retain—still alive, still powerful—the welter of old assumptions about women's nature, and men's. And these assumptions—tying women to the physical, denying the power of their minds—set up stumbling blocks for the advancement of women in any work dependent on the trained mind, which is to say, women in all of the professions.

It is the author's underlying belief that barriers exist where inequalities lie. Barriers are defined as those factors which circumvent or inhibit either the entry or advancement of women into jobs, occupations, and organizations. The purpose of this chapter is to enhance the overall awareness of common barriers which impede the progress of women who seek to advance into higher education administration.

Chapter Four

Barriers to Women's Advancement into Higher Education Administration

Deborah Sims LeBlanc

A THEORETICAL PERSPECTIVE

*P*hilosophically speaking, the key to the removal of barriers for women lies in the provision of justice and equality for all, regardless of race, sex, color, or creed. The professional inequality of women is readily apparent within the academic ranks where they are underrepresented and their salaries are lower than for men (both overall and at every rank). Most would argue that women have faced many barriers in their struggle towards high achievement in all aspects of leadership throughout the ages. But, it is important for those in higher education administration to understand that professional inequality is no longer an acceptable norm in the advancement of women.

> Women are now laying claim to significant and sat-isfying work in the professions as a normal part of their lives and laying claim also to the authority, prestige,

DEBORAH SIMS LeBLANC is the Chair of the Department of Law and Public Administration at National University in San Diego, California. Dr. LeBlanc has taught for the Los Angeles Community College District and California State University, Long Beach. She holds a B.A. in Political Science from California State Polytechnic University, M.P.A. from the University of Southern California, and M.S. in Management and Organizational Behavior and doctorate in Public Administration from the University of LaVerne.

power and salary that professional work commands. They are laying claim, in short, to professional equality, and the breadth of change this signifies can scarcely be overstated.[1]

Barriers to the advancement of women are those factors which circumvent or inhibit their entry into jobs, occupations, and organizations. Barriers are seen in the face of inequality.

ON EQUALITY

Equality is a highly abstract concept which is often given concrete application only controversially and with difficulty. But—in the abstract—equality prevails in respect to all of our fundamental social arrangements. According to Bryan Wilson, these barriers or inequalities relate not only to inherent capacities (i.e., native intelligence, temperament, and physical endowment), but more so to the ineluctable factors (i.e., strength, motivation, meanness of spirit, moral disposition, suggestibility, will-power, etc.). Thus the specific biological or social sources of inequalities remain obscure. Further, "inequalities in all of these respects profoundly affect not only the life-chances of individuals, but also the extent to which they can utilize equal opportunities." Thus, "equality of basic rights in the various departments of life alluded to above are capable either of rather mechanical application or a statement of the rights that the individual should enjoy in respect to what he (or she) might wish to do."[2]

Many would agree that the concept of equality has been generally applied to various aspects of higher education. "In particular, the idea that all who qualify for higher education must be admitted to the university is now widely accepted."[3] It should also become generally accepted for qualified women to advance into higher education administration. There is a definite societal benefit to promoting and enhancing equality and eliminating barriers based on gender. Historically speaking, it has been commonly held that the roles of leader, manager, and administrator have been reserved for men. While women were always capable of fulfilling such roles, it has only been in recent years that women have surfaced as figureheads, and away from a more supportive role. Institutions of higher education must not assume a posture of conformity to be viable, but rather of diversity. Higher education administrative systems must become more open and adaptable, and allow themselves to learn from female administrators rather than assuming that female administrators must conform to established patterns.

MOVING BEYOND THE NORMS

It is time for higher education to strive harder to diversify its administrative ranks; to enlarge the community of socially useful and well-educated women. It is time to move beyond the norms. To overcome barriers to women's advancement we must first understand that an"equal role for women in the organization of society has never been the norm."[4] For the most part, "the sphere in which women are to make their contribution is not merely separate but also less powerful than the public world inhabited by men insofar as their private domain affords women no role in the formulation of public policy, in the shaping of the institutions that in turn largely shape and govern our culture."[5] "The two spheres—private and public—do not carry equal responsibility for the creative molding of the society."[6] Generally speaking when we view women in the public sphere, that is, the workplace, we see their roles as being subordinate to men; for example, female nurses/male doctors, female assistants/male researchers, and female teachers/male principals. "It is true that for over a century there have been women professors, lawyers, doctors, scientists, engineers, and executives, and, with women's suffrage, elected officials as well. But they were clearly exceptions to the norm."[7]

Thus, we now have a situation in which two sets of norms coexist. On the one hand, we have new social and political commitments to individual equality, openness of opportunity, and equal responsibility for men and women, and, on the other, old beliefs in the fact and rightness of inequality—in the fact and rightness of a distinction between men and women in their capacities and proper roles. We retain—still alive, still powerful—the welter of old assumptions about women's nature, and men's. And these assumptions—tying women to the physical, denying the power of their minds—set up stumbling blocks for the advancement of women in any work dependent on the trained mind, which is to say, women in all of the professions.[8]

PRACTICAL IMPLICATIONS

Hiring Conditions for Women in Higher Education

There has been increasing research into the factors that either inhibit or promote the entry of women and ethnic minorities into specific occupations. "This interest derives from the fact that the differential allocation of women, for instance, to positions and organizations helps to account for differences in the earnings of women and men with similar human capital endowments."[9] It has been stated that "sex segregation in the workplace is one of the most visible signs of social inequality."[10] According to author Robert F. Szfran, very little is known about how internal and external influences on the educational institution impact the level of equity in personnel decision making involving salary, recruitment, and promotion.[11]

Researchers Alison Konrad and Jeffrey Pfeffer studied the conditions under which women were hired for managerial positions in higher education administration. Their study utilized data on some 821 educational institutions from the 1978 and 1983 College and University Personnel Association's *Administrative Compensation Survey.* The study focused on both the conditions and factors that encourage the hiring of women and minorities for positions that were previously closed to them and the conditions under which students were most likely to come into contact with female and minority authority figures in nontraditional and nonstereotyped positions.[12] The study focused on the following four conditions on the demand side of the labor market that may affect discrimination and segregation in hiring: (1) relative economic attractiveness of jobs; (2) perceptual biases that are enhanced under conditions of uncertainty; (3) organizational susceptibility to enforcement of the federal guidelines for equal employment opportunity (EEO); and demographic group power.[13]

Their findings suggested the following:

1. *Relative Attractiveness of Jobs.* The supply of labor that is available to organizations has a critical influence on hiring practices; women and minorities are hired more often for lower paying jobs in organizations with lower levels of resources.
2. *Perceptual Biases and Uncertainty.* Jobs and occupations come to be seen as typical and more appropriate for men or women or for minorities or non-minorities. Women and minorities are hired for administrative jobs only when uncertainty in the situation is reduced in some way. The researchers hypothesized that women and minorities would be more likely to be promoted from within than hired from outside the organization.
3. *EEO Enforcement.* Women and minorities are more likely to be hired as administrators in public than in private institutions; women and minorities are more likely to enter nontraditional jobs in public institutions.
4. *Demographic Group Power.* The presence of female and minority decision makers should most likely open, through the hiring process, universities, jobs, and positions that have not traditionally been held by women and minorities.

BARRIERS TO ADVANCEMENT

1. Self-Esteem

One of the greatest barriers to advancement is oneself. As Shakespeare said, "To thine own self, be true." It is paramount that women properly assess their skills and abilities as they continue to search for knowledge and truth.

As a 'woman thinketh,' so is 'she'.[14] It is important that the woman administrator in higher education have a strong sense of self-worth, dignity, and meaningful purpose in her life.

2. Need for Self-Improvement

The general notion of desiring to enhance and improve oneself has far reaching benefits. Self-improvement is essential to an ability to develop and ultimately affect the lives of others.

Self-improvement denotes a posture of humility, which in essence implies that a person has not become self-actualized, and is not all that she is capable of becoming. It implies that there are dimensions and goals yet to accomplish.

3. Limited External Interactions

Many higher education administrators have experienced life only within the confines of their textbooks. Few have substantial life experiences even within the fields in which they lecture and are revered as scholars. Experience gives far greater meaning and definition to the theoretical approaches presented in the textbook.

Many women, particularly minorities and women from lower socio-economic groups, experience difficulty with organizational 'fit' both with their internal and experiential work environments. This difficulty may result from a lack of exposure to and interaction with varied social groups and economic levels. The greater the personal exposure, then the greater the opportunities to understand and communicate with larger and more diverse populations in higher education.

4. Motherhood/Family/Academe—The Balancing Act

According to recent surveys, three out of every five women with children under the age of six are working outside of the home; and approximately 50 percent of mothers are returning to work before their babies are a year old. Managing a home, career, and being an effective parent is difficult. While women's roles and their expectations for their lives have changed, social policy has not. The social support system for women's new roles is not yet in place.[15] Because of the difficulties women encounter in balancing the dual roles of mother and worker, some are foregoing motherhood all together and selecting full-time careers instead; while others are choosing full-time motherhood and no career. As author Tillie Olsen puts it, "Being a mother means being constantly interrupted and continually responsive to the needs of someone else."[16]

The demands of the job and the role of being an effective administrator can be overwhelming and extremely time consuming. Administrators may find themselves working 50-60 hours per week, thereby leaving only a limited amount of time for personal and social activities. According to author A.R. Hochschild, "the classic profile of the academic career is cut to the image of the traditional man with his traditional wife."[17] She further believes that academic women have a difficult time achieving the professional recognition in a campus community because they are competing not just against men, but with the 'head of a small branch industry.' Women do not have a wife at home who will handle housekeeping and child care responsibilities. Nor do they have a wife who devotes a significant portion of her time to her mate's responsibilities. If a woman is married, it is likely that her husband has a career of his own. Professional men are at an advantage over professional women because their wives are more likely to work at nonprofessional or less competitive jobs. It is said that a professorship is a two-person career. When a woman is in the position, it is a one-person career and the one person may be psychologically divided between home and career.[18]

The fundamental concern of equality surrounds the barrier of maternity in higher education. Women need policies and laws that consider their childbearing capability, if they are to equal men's freedom of choice. It is clear that policies and laws can never provide equal success for everyone; "however, laws and the structure of work can provide each individual with an equal opportunity or an equal shot at success."[19]

Because we are all social and emotional creatures, it is important to develop, nurture, and maintain productive family and friend relationships as women climb up the organizational ranks in higher education administration.

5. Issues of Loneliness

It has often been stated that, "it is lonely at the top." But it does not have to be. It is important to understand the dynamics of loneliness; and to identify the advantages and disadvantages of personal isolation within the organization. Why am I alone? How can I create greater opportunities to engage in the lives of others? How much time do I require for productive and creative thought? What are my personal clues that I am becoming a victim of loneliness?

While we each need a certain degree of time to be alone—time to reflect, organize, forecast/project, and to critically analyze and develop our personal and organizational plans and agendas—we must also remember the truism that "no man (or woman) is an island."

6. Limited Political/Business (Organizational) Encounters

"The political culture of academia incorporates the features of organization, individual perception, and process."[20]

For the most part, the higher education environment is rather calm, safe, and apolitical. Certainly there are power struggles, dominant personalities, and special interest groups. However, the overall environment is not generally engulfed in politics or power struggles.

7. *Academics vs. Administration*

"Collegial administrative structures may range from rather simple organizations to ones that are part of a more complex university structure."[21]

Perhaps one of the toughest decisions for many educators is the decision to leave the classroom and go into administration—the 'Peter Principle' at best. Like the 'Peter Principle' many women have proven to be dynamic educators in the classroom. They have established excellent rapport with the students and their peers. They enjoy teaching and serving as part of the faculty. They are innovative and productive faculty members who are able to make things happen in the classroom. These dynamic educators are often excellent researchers and public speakers and are often involved in numerous campus and community service-related committees.

"Administrators must remain flexible enough to respond constantly to the many changing characteristics of their environments while working toward achievement of the goals of their institutions."[22] Women need to develop strong leadership qualities in higher education administration; and may do so by being prepared, being flexible, and increasing efforts towards building consensus.[23]

Whether the faculty member or administrator does all or half of the aforementioned, they all share one similarity—commitment to quality education and a genuine desire to positively impact the lives and careers of their students. For the educator, hard work and dedication to quality education can often result in the offer of an 'administrative' position, which takes her out of the classroom environment that she loved and worked in so effectively. On the other hand, such a person has a wonderful opportunity to be of greater service to the overall college community; and thus have a greater impact on the lives and careers of students, staff, and faculty. It could be argued that as an administrator, this former faculty member will now be able to promote and enhance the overall quality of education within the entire institution. Thus, as an administrator the results may be 'long-range,' as opposed to 'short-range' in academics.[24] Even so, the bottom line is the same—quality in teaching and learning.

8. *Need for Critical Career Path*

"Faculty now have few opportunities to change locales and enhance their status by moving 'up' to a more prestigious institution. Opportunities for professional development also are wanting. Funds for time off, special projects, travel to professional meetings, and other means of renewal are disappearing."[25] However, in recent years there has been an increase in the number of programs designed to help academics. "This development is a direct response to two significant trends—the decrease in academic positions available to new Ph.D.s and restricted opportunities available to established faculty for career growth and advancement."[26]

It is becoming increasingly more important that women who aspire to advance into positions of leadership in higher education should actively plan and develop multi-dimensional career paths. Critical career pathing should identify both long- and short-range plans which address the needs of the total individual, not solely her job-related efforts. These plans should specify goals and objectives that address the following areas: (1) occupational and organizational development/advancement, (2) social skill development, and (3) personal/recreational enhancement. Long-range plans should be strategically developed and cover a 5- to 10-year period. Short-range plans should address plans for 6 months to 5 years. Both the short- and long-range plans should offer two or more viable alternatives in each area.

9. Need for Mentoring

Women need good mentors. Mentoring is critical in meeting a variety of needs for women in higher education administration and can positively impact and enhance their careers.

Women need positive role models, effective listeners, and unbiased feedback. We need constructive suggestions and recommendations that allow room for deviation and individual input. We need the indirect and resourceful guidance that mentoring provides.

10. Need for Internal/External Support Systems (Networking)

It is not uncommon to find limited staff and support services in most colleges and universities, even though the workload is extremely demanding. Women need to develop and maintain effective internal and external support systems to assist them in carrying out their academic responsibilities.

Networking is a key method for establishing a personal system of support. Women should become more involved in networking within the campus setting and outside of the college. It is important that women have key contacts in every level of the organization including the operational, middle-management, and executive management levels, as well as contacts with the board, and significant people in the community outside of the campus.

By establishing and maintaining a strong internal/external support system, a woman becomes more resourceful. The greater her resource-fulness, then the greater her sphere of possible positive influence in higher education.

11. Ability To See the 'Big Picture' Within the Organization

It is critical that women attend board meetings and other key planning and decision-making meetings regularly and get involved in the initial planning phases of major projects and programs. It is para-mount that women are fully aware and involved in overall planning and forecasting of university-wide activities, and yet, as Myra Per-Lee states, we must be apolitical and non-polarized in our efforts.[27]

CONCLUSION

There are numerous barriers to women's advancement into higher education administration; only the surface has been lightly touched in this chapter. Greater attention must be devoted to the development of women's intrapersonal and interpersonal skills if women are to achieve upward mobility.

The author has developed the following list of 12 strengths that, if developed, may assist women in overcoming these barriers to ad-vancement in higher education administration:

1. Excellence in teaching;
2. Research/publication;
3. Campus/community service;
4. Good peer evaluations;
5. Increased global education;
6. Strong personal financial base;
7. Integrity, sound judgment, and effective communication skills; being politically astute;
8. Developing contacts in key governmental and private-sector offices; ability to network and enhance resources;
9. Positive mentor/protege relationships;
10. Personal commitment to quality education;
11. Sense of self-worth and value; social graces; personal and recreational skills (i.e., travel, golf, tennis);
12. Knowledge of budgetary and personnel concerns.

It is time for academia to strive harder to diversify its adminis-trative ranks and overcome barriers to women's advancement in higher education administration, for it is this overall vitality and diversity upon which higher education institutions depend.

ABSTRACT

The workplace, including the college campus, has been less adapt-able than the home in dealing with the changing roles of women. Many employers ignore the fact that their staff members have personal lives whose demands can affect their job performance. Academia often expects faculty members and administrators to be helped by their families in their work, which sounds good in theory but in practice is true for men more often than for women. A working wife is often expected to help her husband's career by attending social functions and packing suitcases for travel, but the reverse is not necessarily true.

This chapter takes a look at the multiple roles women assume and offers practical advice for women, their male colleagues, and the workplace.

Chapter Five

Redesigning the Ivory Tower:
Opening the Drawbridge to Women with Multiple Roles

Bonnie Jones

INTRODUCTION

Colleges and universities across the country cry out in every advertisement for a new administrator, "Women are encouraged to apply." Federal regulation of higher education has forced a change in the application environment for women, but the campus environment today maintains its masculine orientation. Statistics on women in higher education show that colleges and universities are far behind the times. Since 1979 women have made up more than half of higher education's student enrollment, but in 1989 only 11 percent of the chief executive officers of colleges and universities accredited by the six major regional accrediting agencies were women. In fact, a 1982 listing of 52 types of administrative positions with titles of chief officer,

BONNIE JONES is the Associate Dean for Admissions and Educational Research at the Northeastern Ohio Universities College of Medicine (NEOUCOM) in Rootstown, Ohio. She has worked as Registrar, Director of Student Services, and Assistant Dean for Student Affairs at NEOUCOM. In addition, Dr. Jones has published in the area of women's multiple roles and academic performance. She received her B.S. degree in Education from Miami University in Oxford, Ohio, M.Ed. and Ph.D. in Educational Psychology and Higher Education Administration from Kent State University.

dean, or director, had only eight areas in which women held more than 50 percent of the positions: dean of home economics, dean of nursing, bookstore director, affirmative action/equal employment director, payroll manager, director of alumni affairs, director of publications, and director of student placement. Women administrators are clustered at the lowest levels of administration, e.g., 28 percent of the directors of admissions were women in 1987, 50 percent of the associate directors, and 66 percent of the assistant directors. Eisenberg theorized that the reason women are clustered at the lower levels in academia is the extra workload associated with child care and home care—women's multiple roles.[1] Also, men report that being a father has a positive effect on their work, but women (even those without children) feel work has a negative effect on childbearing.[2]

Because female administrators do not fit the stereotypical standard of either their male colleagues or the stay-at-home wives of male administrators, women have been made to feel isolated from the academic mainstream. In the meantime, the male administrators have not been expected to spend overwhelming amounts of time on housekeeping and child care activities. This double standard maintains the status quo in the academic environment, because opportunities for advancement have usually been for men in the upper reaches of the ivory tower, not for women of comparable qualifications. Most executives in upper levels of organizations have never had to balance work and home priorities, because the majority of them have been men who had a wife to handle the personal side of life while they dealt with the work side. Therefore, they cannot understand role conflicts felt by their modern workers, whether male or female. It is usually assumed that family problems are only "women's problems," but as men take on more family responsibility, they feel strain, too. Both men and women with roles beyond the campus must be involved in higher education's future—it needs to be a compilation of values of both men and women, not one or the other.[3]

Women who have multiple roles can be viewed in two ways by higher education. They can be seen as potential risks as administrative candidates because they have too much of a personal life. On the other hand, they can be seen as having rich life experiences with tolerance and understanding of people who work for them. It is fairly easy to add a few words to a job ad; it takes far more effort for colleges and universities to develop the type of environment conducive to the development of women in leadership roles.

STATISTICS ON U.S. WORKING WOMEN

The United States Department of Labor's Women's Bureau compiled figures on working women in 1988. At that time, 56 percent of the female population of 96.5 million was in the labor force. Sixty-five per cent of the 33 million women with children under the age of 18 worked outside the home. Slightly over half of the mothers of infants under one year old worked. About three-fourths of the mothers were married, 9 percent divorced, 8 percent never married, 5 percent had an absent spouse, and 2 percent were widowed. Three-fourths of the divorced mothers worked, 62 percent of the mothers in married couple families worked, and 47 percent of the mothers with absent spouses, widowed, or never married were working. About 56 percent of mothers with children under the age of 6 were in the labor force, and so were 73 percent of mothers with children age 6 and over. In 1978 only 39 percent of mothers with children under age 3 worked. That figure grew to 53 percent in 1988.[4]

Multiple Roles Defined

Most people fulfill several major roles simultaneously in their lives. Within these social positions certain behaviors are considered to be appropriate and even required by observers (colleagues, spouses, children, parents, friends), or the behaviors are imposed by the people in the roles themselves as a result of tradition and family background.[5] In addition to having administrators, campuses are filled with spouses, parents, elderly caregivers, grandparents, friends, and community volunteers. Administrators even find themselves in the roles of chauffeurs, animal trainers, maids, small engine repairers, crisis mediators, holiday banquet caterers, delivery persons, soccer coaches, etc. Whenever a person fulfills several major life roles at once, he or she is a multiple role person.

Depending on the size of the institution, some college administrators fulfill multiple roles within their jobs, too. Multiple titles are fairly common: director of admissions and records; dean for academic and student affairs; assistant vice president for institutional advancement and alumni relations; director of personnel, compensation, and benefits; and associate vice president of accounting, budgeting, and administrative services.

ROLES WOMEN ASSUME BEYOND THE IVORY TOWER'S WALLS

Women's outside roles are often more difficult to shove aside in favor of the job compared to men's outside roles. Both on campus and off campus, an individuals sex role is a part of him or herself, and too often women's sex roles and work roles can become confused on a university campus.[6] Many women are wives and mothers, sometimes single mothers, in addition to being college administrators. The roles of wife and mother usually entail far more household time than the roles of husband and father. Instead of withdrawing from responsibilities in the home and for the children when taking on paid employment, most women simply add to their list of responsibilities.[7] Because women often have less control of their non-work time, they are at a disadvantage in higher education as compared to men. If a man has a project that is under a deadline, he can wait a few days to change the oil in the car. However, if a woman does not change a baby's diapers immediately, a real emergency could occur!

Even though men are more likely nowadays to have a working wife, the majority of them have not changed their lifestyles very drastically from their father's lifestyles of the 1950s. *Attitudes* may have changed about sharing child care, household, and elder care tasks, but the *behaviors* have not changed. When polled, 50 percent of men believed that they should share domestic work when their wives were employed, but few actually did share 50-50 in housework and child care with their wives.[8] The biological fact that women bear children will not change, and this fact has shaped traditional sex roles through the centuries. Yet by age 40, 90 percent of executive men are fathers, and only 35 percent of executive women have children. Therefore, automatically assuming that children will interfere with work is not justified. Schwartz further argued that, except for childbearing, both men and women are capable of a full range of behaviors—aggression, nurturance, competition, support, self-reliance, and sensitivity—androgyny is here, and yet many CEOs still see careers as inherently masculine and parenting as inherently feminine.[9]

Professional women in equalitarian marriages (shared household and child care responsibilities) were found to be more likely to continue working after having children, but the women also spent more time alone with their children than their husbands did. Women in this study reported spending 18 hours alone with their children per week, while their husbands spent seven hours. Husbands of non-working wives spent six hours per week alone with their children. It appears that equality means that the woman shares in the responsibility of earning money, but the husband does not necessarily share in child care responsibilities. In the same study, husbands of full-time working wives actually spent almost the same amount of time alone with their children as husbands of non-employed wives. Women did report that a supportive husband permitted them to be a career success after having a child.[10]

A corporate study of 711 employees was conducted by Googins and Burden to determine if there were differences in the home demands of various groups of workers. They calculated the average number of hours per week that employees spent on-the-job and in household tasks and child care. The number of hours spent at work for men and women did not vary much, with the numbers ranging from 39 to 44 hours per week. The major differences were found in the amount of time spent on home chores and child care. Married female parents spent

40 hours at work, and an additional 45 hours in home chores and child care. Married male parents spent 44 hours at work, 14 hours in child care, and 11 hours in household chores if their wife worked but 12 hours if she did not work! In fact, men with an employed wife had an increase in income and did less work at home—the best of both worlds.[11] These figures dramatically show that women on the job and men on the job do not have the same support systems at home.

Yogev studied 164 faculty women's reported time spent on their professions, their children, and their housework. Women who had children had a total work week on the average of 107 hours, about two and a half full-time jobs, compared to women without children who worked an average of 78 hours per week, about two full-time jobs. Because there are only 168 hours per week, a married faculty member with children had only 4.42 hours left per week to spend on herself after allowing time for sleep. Surprisingly though, Yogev reported that the mothers felt no more overloaded by work than the childless faculty women, possibly because they consider child care enjoyable rather than a burden. Yogev also reported another possible explanation. Because these women grew up with sex-role stereotypes of the mother staying at home and the father working, perhaps they did not want to admit that they were overworked. They believed that they had chosen the tougher path in life, and to complain about it would be to admit failure to make the right decision or inadequacy in fulfilling both home and work roles. Yogev stressed that the gap between the subjective reports of the faculty women and the objective listing of hours spent in work activities signaled a problem in helping women deal with their pressures. Until women admit that there is a problem, no solutions to their workload will be forthcoming.[12]

Publicity and research on women's multiple roles often focuses on younger women, but there has been an increase in the number of middle-aged women working. Divorce, fewer children at home to care for, labor saving devices, and increased educational levels are the reasons for the influx of middle-aged women into the work force. Elder care is a responsibility for an estimated 25 percent of the U.S. workforce, and there is a growing elderly population who are dependent. It is more likely a daughter or daughter-in-law who takes care of the needs of elderly parents, not because the sons do not care, but because that is the way our culture has assigned the roles. Middle-aged women who care for both children and their elderly parents are described as "women in the middle." These women feel in the middle because they are being pressured from two value systems—the traditional value that says they should care for the elderly family members and the more modern value that women should be free to choose to work outside the home. Gibeau and Anastas found that role conflict for working women providing elder care was greater if they also had children at home.[13] In studies by Brody and her colleagues, employed and non-employed daughters provided almost equal amounts of care to their elderly mothers with a mean of 35 hours per week of elder care.[14] Here is another example of women taking on more tasks when they work rather than replacing tasks.

A discussion of whether or not there is also a "third shift" for women has started in the popular press. In her book, *The Beauty Myth: How Images of Female Beauty Are Used Against Women*, Naomi Wolf claimed that working women are expected to look like a magazine photo of career women while handling all their roles—what she called the PBQ, Professional Beauty Qualification. Women spend time and money on diets, cosmetic surgery, and beauty products to the detriment of their self esteem.[15]

MULTIPLE ROLES AS MOATS PREVENTING ADVANCEMENT

Role Overload and Role Conflict

When people perceive that they must perform too many tasks and too many demands and expectations are put on them, they suffer from role overload. Administrators have multiple sources telling them how to carry out their individual roles. If all of these sources are sending the same signals about how an individual should act, the individual should succeed. However, if these signals are different (e.g., supervisor wants female to work overtime, husband wants wife to work but be home when he is, mother says wife should stay home with child like she did), role conflict results. Role conflict is defined as "the concurrent appearance of two or more incompatible expectations for the behavior of a person."[16] How college administrators perceive the role expectations placed on them by a supervisor, a spouse, a parent, or a child impacts on the amount of conflict that occurs and the amount of strain that results.

Intrarole conflict results when pressures within a single life role develop, perhaps because a person's characteristics are incompatible with the requirements of the role, whether at work or at home. Interrole conflict, as defined by Barling and MacEwen is "the extent to which a person experiences pressures within one role that are incompatible with the pressures that arise in another role."[17]

Role conflict has been found to be higher in women than in men.[18] Greenhaus and Beutell defined work-family conflict as a "form of interrole conflict in which the role pressures from the work and family domains are mutually incompatible in some respect. That is, participation in the work (family) role is made more difficult by participation in the family (work) role."[19] The conflict may be because of time problems with inflexibility or conflicts in scheduling, because of emotional strains from children or spouse, or because of behaviors required in one domain that are not effective in the other domain. In a study of role conflict between work and home, Burke concluded that work-family (interrole) conflict had a greater effect on stress levels than within work or within family conflicts (intrarole conflicts) for both men and women. Therefore, although women may feel more interrole conflict, men experience it, too. In addition, males may start feeling the effects of interrole conflicts as they take on more extra-work responsibilities and their wives enter the workforce. Problems of one family member usually affect all family members in some way.[20]

Gray surveyed 232 married women doctors, lawyers, and professors regarding their multiple roles and coping methods. Almost half of the women said they could not choose between the importance of family and career roles and that they often experienced role conflict. Nevertheless, the assumption should not be made automatically that occupying multiple roles leads to role conflict. Being successful in one life role can develop strengths that make a person successful in another life role. Gray concluded that a combination of family and work was rewarding for women if they developed effective coping strategies.[21]

Effects of Multiple Roles

Studies have tried to determine whether or not involvement in multiple roles is helpful or harmful to women's health and life satisfaction, and the results are inconclusive. There are so many variables to take into consideration for each individual that many studies have not been able to control for all of them. In a review of the literature on women's multiple roles and their effects on mental and physical health, Froberg, et al. claimed that women who occupy several roles enjoy better health than women with few roles. Nevertheless, there are exceptions to this claim depending on the roles being occupied and the woman's perception of the quality of the roles. No longer are researchers as concerned about the number of roles that women occupy; now they are analyzing specific combinations, patterns, and characteristics of the roles of women.[22]

Barnett and Baruch concluded that being a paid worker did not necessarily lead to role strain, role overload, or role conflict. Instead, the balance (or imbalance) between rewards and stressors perceived by the women themselves predicted negative or positive effects. It is not the number of roles that a woman takes on, but the quality of those roles that causes strain or satisfaction. Coverman argued that time spent at home and at work had few psychological consequences for women, because they have developed strategies to accommodate their multiple role demands. However, if they saw their roles as conflicting, they suffered from psychological distress. Therefore, role overload itself is not damaging, but women's perceptions of role conflict are. Repetti et al. agreed that being employed does not necessarily mean negative effects on women's health, particularly if the woman is unmarried or is married and has favorable work attitudes. The reasons cited for this beneficial effect of work were opportunities for increased social support from co-workers and supervisors and increased income. However, negative effects have also been observed, and include somatization, depression, anxiety, obsessive compulsiveness, discomfort, anger/hostility, and dissatisfaction.[23]

Employment status alone did not change predictors of marital satisfaction for women in the postparental period. Women's outside employment can even reduce some negative marital stress, but it does not appear to increase or decrease stress associated with the child care role.[24]

Findings from Barnett and Baruch's study suggest that the greatest role strain and anxiety occurs when the woman is a mother. Among the male employees in the Googins and Burden corporate study, married male parents with employed wives were at the highest risk for depression and reported the largest number of days absent from work per year. Therefore, both dual career spouses with children are vulnerable to role strain. For women, it seems to show up in extra hours of the total work load; for men, it may mean less emotional support from the wife who has little extra time to take care of the husband's needs.[25] Yet, if men spent more time on household tasks and child care, they would probably start to show the stress and strain of this extra work time. Equal sharing of the duties may somewhat ease the strain on the wife, but may make the husband's stressors worse. Therefore, an equitable sharing of the tasks is not the full answer.

TACTICS USED TO COPE WITH MULTIPLE ROLES

Effective interrole coping can mean either reducing personal stress or improving the situation.[26] The coping methods used by women in multiple roles can be categorized through the following schema: surrendering to the roles, developing personal strategies to reduce the stress of the roles, and restructuring the roles themselves.

Surrendering

Some women deal with the multiple role issue by surrendering to the situation, either by avoiding taking on multiple roles or by not allowing themselves to admit problems. In a study of 135 college faculty women, 29 percent used reactive role behavior to cope with role conflicts. They tried to work harder at pleasing everyone and had no conscious strategy to control the demands or their responses. Another 4 percent withdrew from roles and made decisions that they either would not be able to marry or would not have children if they worked. Still another 4 percent became defensive, either by telling themselves that they should not feel the way they do or by blaming the situation or others.[27] O'Neill and Zeichner found a strong relationship between the way women cope with job stress and their psychological and physical health. Women in their study who used avoidance as a coping strategy reported higher depression, anxiety, and physical symptoms. Holahan and Moos found that using avoidance coping techniques resulted in negative psychological consequences to life stress.[28]

Hochschild described one working wife who supposedly used the technique of changing her thinking about the situation. She balanced the large amount of work she did in her home with the relatively little her husband did by dividing the house into the downstairs (garage and basement) and the upstairs (everything else). Her husband took care of the downstairs and the dog, and she took care of the upstairs and their child. Cognitively rethinking her situation made the work equally distributed to her, even though it was not in actuality. This cognitive reappraisal of the situation was used by only 1 percent of the women in a study of college faculty. Some women will compartmentalize tasks by keeping work problems at work and home problems at home. Is this always possible? Women who avoid the problems of multiple roles find that their method does not work and their functioning becomes impaired.[29]

Strategizing

Some women will develop strategies to handle multiple roles without lessening the demands of the roles in any way. The stress of the roles may be managed through getting up earlier or staying up later at night to get everything done, managing time more efficiently, enrolling in time management workshops, and engaging in some form of exercise or relaxation to dissipate the stress. Programs emphasizing relaxation and desensitization have been found to be equally as effective in reducing stress as instructional programs in time management, rational-emotive therapy, and assertiveness training. Women in multiple roles are always juggling tasks, running errands on lunch hours, and prioritizing work demands and home demands. Obviously, being as organized as possible and avoiding time wasters, like waiting in lines, help make daily lives easier. It takes a great deal of planning to get the required tasks done, but most women also require "their own time" to unwind, whether that be at aerobics, through reading, or working on a hobby. Unfortunately, some women will not even do this, because they see taking care of themselves as one more role burden and they are last on their own priority list.[30]

Group counseling is another method to help lesson women's stress of multiple roles and sense of isolation. Gilbert and Rachlin claimed that women are often unaware how stressed they are, because they have just accepted it. These two researchers recommend counselors help women recognize stress and its physical and emotional aspects and instruct them on good nutrition, exercise, time management, and values clarification. Amatea and Fong-Beyette found that only 2 percent of the faculty women in their study sought out moral support rather than solutions or information for their multiple role problems. Stanford University developed an eight-week luncheon group for professional women on campus who were juggling multiple roles in an effort to live up to the superwoman myth. The women shared their unrealistic expectations of themselves, gave each other individual support, broadened their awareness of the issue, and shared successful coping methods. The group built friendships, mentoring networks, and a sense of pride in the participants. This type of program may be the first step in recognizing multiple roles for women and could be the grass roots group to start activity on campus toward making environmental changes. Programs to help women with multiple roles will not cut down on their time demands but will help them become more realistic in their expectations for themselves.[31]

Restructuring

Long interviewed 20 professional women about their coping strategies and concluded that the more effective copers took problem-solving action and the less effective copers just used resigned acceptance of the situation. Modifying the source or circumstances of stress with multiple roles can be an effective coping mechanism, but also one with which women feel most uncomfortable. Their expectation for themselves is that they are on call for everyone else 24 hours a day. Most women have been brought up to believe that they will be taken wrongly if they assert themselves or say no. Women who have a difficult time describing how they really feel often become resentful and should seek out a course in assertiveness training. The inequitable home work load in most households probably came about by default, because over the years women have not asserted their concerns about fairness. About 37 percent of the faculty women in Amatea and Fong-Beyette's study dealt with their multiple roles by redefining them either internally or externally. Internally, they reset their own priorities and modified their standards. Externally, they sought out additional resources to help them (babysitters, housekeepers) or reallocated the roles to other family members. Negotiating family responsibilities and arriving at consensus about standards for household tasks requires open communication, something that may be lacking in many dual career households with several children. Therefore, a conscious effort must be made to communicate. Women also need to learn delegation skills rather than relying on themselves to do everything. Delegating can reduce administrators' strains while at the same time offering opportunities for other staff members to gain self-esteem and recognition. Delegating household tasks to babysitters, caterers, housekeepers, and shopping services is the mark of most successful women lawyers, and probably of successful women college administrators. When a woman recognizes that her life can be more enjoyable by making a few modifications, she often feels greater internal locus of control and less role overload.[32] She feels in control of her life and time rather than feeling that others are controlling her.

In their study of 69 multiple role women, McLaughlin et al. concluded that women who had the ability to use multiple coping strategies were less likely to allow distress to build up to the point of negatively affecting their marital relationships. Women who actively problem solved and tried to change their work environments were able to lessen the effects of stress on their lives.[33]

LADDERS FOR SCALING THE WALLS

Redesigning the Ivory Tower

Upper-level administrators can be urged by other administrators to take on the task of balancing work and family life for faculty, staff, and students.[34] For a campus environment to be conducive to faculty and staff fulfilling multiple roles, there needs to be a campus aura of support for work and family that permeates all departments at all levels. It is a copout for a human resources office or the president to expect a single campus committee on family concerns to be responsible for suggesting and making all of the improvements.

Nearly every office on campus can provide some form of assistance to faculty and staff fulfilling multiple roles. Not only would services benefit the individuals, they also could benefit the departments. Examples of activities that enhance the environment for faculty and staff in multiple roles are listed in Figure 1. Creative and committed campuses can develop many more. In a shrinking economy, college and university departments could earn extra income from providing these services in addition to providing jobs for local residents. Some of these tactics also offer enrolled students an opportunity to earn extra income and gain experience in their chosen careers.

Even though campuses have already implemented children's activities and services, they sometimes are scheduled at times that are more convenient for the department than for potential users. For example, a day care program through the Family Studies Department may run on Tuesdays from 9:30 to 11:30 a.m. This time period may be convenient for mothers who are not employed, but not for working mothers and fathers. Likewise, summer enrichment programs may be

Figure 1

Practical Tactics for Redesigning the Ivory Tower

Academic Departments: Summer-long enrichment programs for elementary and middle school children in art, music, science, math, computers, geography, geology, history, literature, drama, dance, and languages with lunch provided and child care available at 7:30 a.m. and until 5:30 p.m. to accommodate working parents. Reduced costs for children of university faculty and staff.

Athletic Department: Summer sports camps at reduced rates for faculty and staff children with child care available before and after starting times.

College of Education: Child learning centers, home babysitting referral services, evening and weekend child care center. These can be offered to the entire community, but at a discount for faculty and staff.

College of Nursing: Provide in-home nurses aides for ill children and elderly parents of faculty and staff.

Financial Office: Revised travel policies that include reimbursement for telephone calls home to check on children and overnight child care expenses.

Food Service: Provide pickup service for nightly dinners or holiday dinners, like Thanksgiving dinner.

Gerontology Center: Referral list and analysis of services provided by elderly group homes, nursing homes, and home health care agencies in the area.

Governmental Affairs: State and federal lobbying assistance to local agencies interested in multiple roles.

Grants Office: Identify sources of funding for helping women and men in multiple roles and referring those sources to appropriate departments for program development or research on the topic.

Groundskeeping: Referral list of groundskeepers who will mow lawns, cut shrubbery, rake leaves, etc. on weekends and evenings at faculty and staff homes. This list could include those who have applied for this type of position at the college or university, but there have not been openings for all of them.

Health Center: Reserve an area for mildly ill children of faculty and staff to prevent lost work days.

Housekeeping: Referral list of housekeepers in residence halls who are willing to work during the summer for faculty and staff when residence halls are closed; laundry and ironing services for faculty and staff.

Human Resources: Campus policies on flex-time, job sharing, summer hours, work-at-home, extended maternity and paternity leave, adoptive parent leave, personal leave; revised benefit policies that include child care and elder care subsidies; contracts with local agencies and businesses for child care and elder care.

Library: Saturday morning or afternoon movies and reading circles for children of faculty and staff with student supervision to enable parents to grocery shop, run errands, shop for Christmas gifts, etc.

Music Department: After-school music program at elementary schools in the service area. Parents can pick up children after 5 p.m.

Psychology Department and Counseling Center: Support groups, workshops, and personal counseling on handling multiple roles; phone lines for children of faculty and staff to call after school to check in.

Purchasing Department: Referral lists for major purchases, bulk items, or discounts for college and university faculty and staff.

School of Technology: Repairs of small engines and appliances, home remodeling work, auto maintenance.

Transportation Service: Pick up children of faculty and staff at local elementary schools for after-school programs on campus.

scheduled from 9 a.m. to 3 p.m. without having day care before or after to accommodate working parents.

As on most campuses, the response to women by corporations has been cosmetic and symbolic, more to avoid litigation than anything else. Because being a mother causes the most stress for women, providing child care has been suggested as the primary ingredient to aiding working women. Women are much more satisfied with their lives if they feel comfortable with the child care arrangements. Academicians, though are penalized for being parents and fringe benefit packages need to include day care as readily as health care in order for balance to be achieved between males and females in professional roles. A study in the summer of 1987 by the Bureau of Labor Statistics of 10,000 business establishments revealed that only 11 percent of them offered direct benefits such as employer-sponsored day care, child care cost assistance, child care information and referral, and counseling services. About three-fourths offered flex-time, flexible leave, and voluntary part-time schedules. Many companies interviewed for a study on family-supportive policies claimed that the first time they ever considered family needs of workers was when a suggestion was made to provide an on-site day-care facility. The suggestion was usually turned down and no other alternatives or issues discussed because of a misconception that a day-care center was the only solution to providing family support. Sensitization to work-family concerns never materialized.[35] While day care is a problem for a number of administrators, both male and female, it is not the only problem that needs attention. Family issues are much more complex and far-reaching.

Women administrators' salaries are not at parity with men's and the entire benefit system is set up from a male perspective. If women are the home partners who hire the housekeepers and nannies, they need to be paid enough money to afford these services. Instead, the national averages from 1987-88 show that in every single administrative position, males make a higher average salary than females for the same job title. Higher education is not unique in this disparity; it is found in corporations, too. According to an Associated Press analysis of United States census figures, in 1980 women earned 62 percent of what men did and by 1991 women were earning 72 percent. This so-called increase is more a result of men's wages going down in our current economy rather than women's wages going up.[36]

Colleges and universities defend their salary figures by stating that women do not have as many years experience as men in the same positions. However, in the few cases where women do have more years experience than men (i.e., 6 years for men and 12 years for women as dean of home economics) or the same number of years experience (i.e., 8 years for both as dean of nursing), the average male salary is still higher.[37]

With the heightened awareness of sexual harassment as a result of the 1991 confirmation hearings of Supreme Court Justice Clarence Thomas, colleges and universities must clarify men's and women's work roles to avoid conflict and ambiguity. This clarification will decrease the possibility of a person's sex role and work role becoming confused.[38]

Suggestions for Ladies In Waiting

Healy and Welchert introduced a contextual-developmental theory of mentoring that actually combines the strengths of women in multiple roles. Multiple role women are often successful at both work and home as a result of blending leadership and nurturant characteristics. Healy and Welchert's view of mentoring is one of ". . . a dynamic, reciprocal, relationship in a work environment between an advanced career incumbent (mentor) and a beginner (protege) aimed at promoting the career development of both."[39] During the process of mentoring the protege develops a style and wisdom similar to the mentor's, but the protege also provides the mentor with feedback, fresh ideas, and new approaches that also improve the mentor's reputation. It seems as if Healy and Welchert are describing parenthood with its continued opportunities with reciprocity in this form of mentoring. Women may be less likely than men to view mentoring (and parenthood) as a one-way process of training the young. Instead it is a dynamic situation in which both the mentor (mother) and the protege (child) learn and develop from each other. Women should not just mentor women either. The campus stereotypes will not break down until women administrators are viewed as mentors to both males and females.

When subordinates are viewed as peers, a different type of leadership emerges, too. Women in leadership positions have the opportunity to generate future women leaders. Sagaria and Johnsrud described a type of leadership in which women staff and students around them become more empowered through mutual respect. Generative leadership goes one step beyond participatory leadership. People do not just participate in decision making under generative leadership. They also are given the opportunity to learn and practice becoming leaders themselves. Collaboration, productivity, consensus, and creativity are promoted, and the unique talents of each member of a working group are highly valued and used. The generative leadership style also offers women a way to delegate gracefully. Everyone is valued and has responsibility to the group, and therefore is required to perform tasks that under other leadership styles might be done only by the leader.[40]

On a practical level, women administrators need to admit limitations and let professionals handle household tasks. Get cookies at the bakery, find a weekly or biweekly cleaning service, take more clothes to the dry cleaners, and hire a caterer for special dinners in your home. Women need to allow fathers and grandparents to handle some responsibilities, like child care, grocery shopping, children's doctor appointments, etc. They, too, get a sense of pride from handling these stereotypical motherly tasks. Children need their independence. Have them pack their own school lunches, close their bedroom doors rather than cleaning, and teach older children how to do laundry.

In My Dreams . . . Suggestions for Male Administrators

If any male administrators read this chapter, my dreams for the future of the ivory tower would include giving them some practical advice: (1) Include both male and female subordinates in all office activities—from special presentations to the Board of Trustees down to daily lunch plans. (2) Be supportive of women (and men) who offer suggestions for making the campus more amenable to people handling multiple roles. Don't just say it is a good idea; do something to help implement it. (3) Be brave enough to check your office's salary schedule to verify that you have not inadvertently been paying men more than women. A simple listing of your staff in descending salary order by name, sex, job title, years of experience, and degrees held may reveal some interesting discrepancies. (4) Finally, if you are married, instead of "helping out" at home, take total responsibility for some household tasks your wife especially dislikes. For many working women this would be a far more meaningful anniversary gift than jewelry or flowers. Support from husbands has also been shown to be a way to reduce interrole conflict in employed mothers and improve marital functioning.[41]

Future Research

The anecdotal evidence that women are juggling multiple roles is extensive, but rather than just counting the burdens, systematic analysis of relationships of roles and individual reactions are needed to understand the moderators of stress. Research needs to look at multiple variables in both the roles and the individuals. Confounding effects are also present in the existing research, e.g. most studies do not distinguish between women in high versus low prestige occupations. There has also been a lack of analysis of racial/ethnic factors that may moderate or exacerbate the strain of women's multiple roles. Although most effects of multiple roles occur over time, the research to date has been mostly cross-sectional rather than longitudinal.[42] Longitudinal research would be valuable in analyzing trends and long-term consequences.

Finally, the research has been sparse on the coping methods of multiple role women in higher education administration. Data could be collected from college and university administrators through several national professional organizations and shared with their members. The experiences of women in higher education administration might be quite different from managerial women in corporations or even women faculty members.

CONCLUSION

Although American lifestyle preference is now some combination of work and family, the traditional view prevails that these two domains have conflicting rather than shared values. There is no national family policy that recognizes how diverse the American family is and that offers flexibility in meeting their needs, both economically and socially. Mounting information has documented that the problem of integrating multiple roles is reaching serious proportions, and yet no group has emerged to assume a leadership role in responding to these concerns.[43] What better place than a college or university campus to take the lead in making it easier for men and women alike to integrate these two vital roles. As educational and research institutions, campuses owe it to society and to the dedicated women who work for them to be the forerunners in comprehending and embracing multiple roles and then teaching our children how best to function in both work and family worlds. These two institutions—the campus and the home—should no longer be considered to be mutually exclusive in our American society, whether you are a man or a woman. In 1981, Brody called for a "revised contract," not just between men and women, but between American society and the family as a whole.[44] Let's not wait too long.

ABSTRACT

The following scripts are brief vignettes similar to the lives of thousands of working women. The success of these women in all areas of their lives depends on careful analysis and planning. Until now, very little has been written about how women can conquer the conflicting issues that confront them in their personal and professional arenas. Imitating the management style of their fathers, husbands, and brothers has proved unsatisfactory. Perceptions of women's roles in society are slowly changing as today's woman is becoming a valued resource in the work force. In conjuction with this change, women are beginning to develop their own management styles.

This chapter illustrates how the successful woman administrator creates a blueprint for personal ownership and professional growth. She is the architect of her future, creating all the changes, building upon personal beliefs and prior experiences, shaping her life by purposes and principles—all a part of a vision that is nothing less than reaching for the stars.

Chapter Six

Women Administrators' Emerging Personal and Professional Concerns

Lindalee Ausejo

SINGLE: A DAY IN THE LIFE OF THE FEMALE ADMINISTRATOR

5:30 A.M. *The alarm goes off . . . voices in the background . . . intertwining with a dream—something to do with the Founder's Day Spree being planned for tomorrow afternoon. I hit the 10 minute salvation button on the radio and the silence gives me a few minutes' reprieve.*

5:40 A.M. *I'm up . . . hitting the button on the television. (The TV goes off every night at 11:30 pm as the last scene of "Cheers" cuts across the screen. I love those timers.)*

5:45 A.M. *A splash of cool water to my face, my hair rolled in steam curlers, I gather my papers together (which are strewn all over the study), placing them in the well-used briefcase. The dog, hearing my movements, yips a hello. Food and a loving hug is on the way.*

LINDALEE AUSEJO is the Principal of Wilson Elementary School in Richmond Unified School District, California. She has also worked as the coordinator of the Human Relations Department. Dr. Ausejo has been an instructor at the College of Marin, the University of San Diego, and St. Mary's College, and the Leadership Development National Center for Employment Studies, University of San Francisco. She holds B.A. and M.A. degrees from California State University at San Francisco, M.S. from California State University at Hayward, and an Ed.D. in Organization and Leadership from the University of San Francisco.

6:00 A.M.   I scan the agendas for the day, personal and profes-
            sional, to focus on my first task. Nothing until 7:30
            am. Good! I grab the vacuum and clean the first floor
            of the three-story rambling stone Swiss structure I call
            home. Menial tasks always have to be squeezed in
            between jobs, meetings, and social activities. Vacuum-
            ing is one of these.

6:20 A.M.   No time for breakfast . . . that is an excuse. I don't
            enjoy breakfast 'til the weekend arrives. Food is never
            a top priority. I look into my walk-in closet. Appro-
            priately color coordinated with everything easily placed
            to grab quickly—tops with bottoms, blouses, sweaters,
            suits, dresses—but slacks are my favorite. Easy to wear.
            Sleek to the eye. Being always in public view, I have
            to be aware of the social protocol in appearance.
            Accessories, lots—hats being my favorite and my
            extravagance—antique jewelry; one couldn't have too
            much. My hand reaches for my newest acquisition—
            a cameo fashioned at the turn of the century. A hand
            knit sweater that looks superb over wool pants. Two
            pairs of shoes—one for walking and one for professional
            situations.

6:30 A.M.   I take great pride in the time it takes me to prepare
            in the morning. I average fifteen minutes to dress, do
            make-up, and run a comb through my hair.

6:45 A.M.   I hit the "on" button to my answering machine—just
            in case somebody can't get in touch with me at work.
            Our lines are forever busy. I say good-bye to my dog—
            asking her to watch the house. She barely raises her
            head from her bed. She acknowledges my going with
            a yawn, feeling comfortable knowing that my
            housemates are still upstairs asleep. (They are an asset
            in helping to pay the mortgage.)

6:55 A.M.   I put the key in the ignition of my little sports car, one
            minute to warm it up and eight minutes more, I meet
            with my friends. Six mornings a week we gather to walk
            for exercise two or three miles. Mall-walking. Safe and
            secure. A real commitment to each other let alone our
            bodies. Guilt sets in lest we not make it. Today, my
            normal hour walk is cut in half.

7:29 A.M.   One minute to spare. My first meeting of the day is
            over a hot cup of tea—my associate is always on time.
            A much respected member of the business community
            and also a personal supporter, Hal is appreciated. He
            is always in my corner. I do whatever I can to assist
            him and the corporation he represents. This world
            would be a much better place if individuals worked

in collaboration and not in competitive turmoil. But perhaps then, our American culture wouldn't be so identifiable.

Today's topic of conversation is my newly appointed position as vice-president of a local organization which is going through a restructuring period. He is concerned that I may get caught up in the political nuances; tread lightly. I say I will and promise to be cautious. Dry toast and a second cup of tea bathed in milk is all I can manage before I leave.

8:25 A.M.   *Students are already waiting as I pull up in front of the school. They greet me with a good morning, a wave, or by simply approaching the car offering to help me with the books, briefcase, purse, whatever I am carrying. Kids are amazing—you can give so little and receive so much in return . . . the keys are love, respect and high expectations. If you have all three ingredients and a healthy mind, you can accomplish anything.*

8:30 A.M.   *A full day ahead. Managing a school encompasses all the "people skills" . . . for 90 percent of my time is involved with the children, their families, the teachers, community members . . . demands are a 'constant.' I am the mediator, the facilitator in managing a school of 565 children from all cultural, ethnic, and religious backgrounds. I find myself involved in peoples' personal and professional lives—helping to make their lives work more easily.*

During the most difficult time of stress I am expected to be the rock of Gibraltar—and this is a given. No time is allotted to my personal needs—and there is never enough time in the day for everything. Our days are never dull . . . I seldom find time to sit.

11:30 A.M.   *Lunch is taken with the students as I oversee the lunchroom . . . the highlight of my day. This is my opportunity to touch the children both physically in a loving caress and mentally in guiding them in social manners. I feel like a surrogate mother; oftentimes there is only one parent in the home. And when there is one—that parent may have other responsibilities and be somewhere else. The school is now a holistic caretaker for its children.*

My own hunger may be satisfied with an apple, perhaps half a sandwich, but always a diet coke. But that's okay—less food and less sitting mean less problems with weight watching.

1:00 P.M.   *The school runs smoothly . . . strong policies, stronger* expectations of the parents; curriculum and programs in place with an excellent teaching staff . . . and a supportive office staff that can now manage itself. Work has always been fun—but it has taken much energy and professional attention to put it into place. Yet, I have always needed a challenge to push myself. My school is always top priority. Oftentimes, my own personal life is set aside if a school activity or a meeting relating to education arises. My friends are always understanding . . . but dates seldom are. The only dates who understand my situation are men who also are in top management positions, especially those who have ownership in their companies; lawyers who are on a case; or a surgeon who is on call. A relationship is difficult to sustain.

2:53 P.M.   School is out . . . but only for the kids. My work day is only half over. I have a project and a deadline to meet. Federal monies were being allocated for schools. I knew we qualified . . . but our central office statistics said no. Going through documentation, student records, into the classrooms interviewing every child in the school and calling homes, I gathered the statistics on each student's grade level, mode of transportation to school, racial background, parental status (single vs. two parents) and lunch program (free vs. partial vs. full payment). I need to complete my accumulation of statistical data and get the results to my Associate Superintendent tomorrow at 8:30 am. This means $50,000—$70,000 towards our Language Arts/Reading/Writing Program. The project is tedious and time consuming but worth it because I know my school population—and I learned a long time ago—taking risks was simply a game to me; yet, I always made very sure of myself before I committed my time and energy; precious commodities. Consequently, those who know me seldom wager.

Over the next two hours and a dozen interruptions I worked the numbers.

5:00 P.M.   I look at the clock—ahhh . . . I need a break. I ring for my custodian—on a regular basis we discuss the necessary maintenance and plant concerns. At the moment we are dealing with a large pipe breakage at our childcare center. Twenty-four hours has passed and still no repair has been made. He always does the maintenance calling—unless it is not attended to by the central office—and then he approaches me for support. My calls are commonly followed by a memo. As a result, action by the central office is quick in *coming. The maintenance department is always very supportive. My custodians love it. I would smile at the quickness of the results and deny the masculine assumption that I was having an affair with someone of power in the district.*

Being single is not much of an asset when one is climbing the "corporate" ladder; sometimes people still hold on to the antiquated belief that "she" may be sleeping around to get what "she" wants. It is all very amusing to me. I really enjoy being a woman—knowing my intelligence/common sense level and at the same time being able to use and handle it wisely. I challenge most men—only because they don't know how to deal with me or because they can't handle themselves. Some would say it's through intimidation. But it is simply, me! I wouldn't know how to be anyone else.

6:00 P.M. *My last phone call of the day. One of my associates just became the newest member of the city council. She and I were planning to meet at one of the local restaurants for a salad. And of course, the ubiquitous diet coke. No dessert. And this restaurant is known for them. Oh well.*

7:30 P.M. *With a light meal under my belt—I head to the gym. Sometimes, I manage to get there at 5:30 am (if I had an earlier evening the night before). On the way I drive past the six-plex that I own, manage, and play "handyman" to every other weekend. Everything seems clean and quiet. Several times a month I would take a drive down to the Monterey peninsula where I have a second home (which I also rent out). There were constantly things to attend to in my "portfolio."*

Doing physical work adds a valuable dimension to my life. I love working in the yard, recreating a new interior to a room, or simply making my environment a more comfortable one in which to live. I do this at school . . . in my apartment complex, and at my homes (the work ethic is part of me). It gives me balance in life. Professional negative stress is minimized—life is too short!

9:00 P.M. *All showered, with hair washed after my workout— I arrive home, hang my clothes, gather another pile together for a morning wash, grab a book, my dog, and climb into bed. I glance over at the desk where my next week's lecture lays. It can wait. On Monday night I teach College English at the State Penitentiary. Talk about fun—now that is fun. I faintly remember promising the inmates I would bake them brownies the next time. I groan. How do I get myself into these situations!*

Cooking is my least favorite chore! I fully believe that early childhood decisions of gender division had a definite impact on me. At five I resented my mother doing all the cooking—it took so long to prepare and so little time to enjoy. It just didn't make sense. If I ever do decide to settle down, I hope that man will enjoy cooking or he will have to live on salads. I would build the house instead.

This is not the man my mother told me about . . . thinking of my mother . . . I reflect on the closeness of our relationship. First thing in the morning I will phone her. (I am fortunate. She lives only 40 minutes away and we see each other at least two or three times a month.)

11:00 P.M. *I push the T.V. button. Have you noticed how many buttons we push daily! Time for "Cheers." One always needs to have a hearty laugh before sleeping a solid six hours. There is no room in my world for the oppressing evening news. There has to be a correlation between sleeping restfully and the news at 11:00. The news can wait until 5:40 am.*

11:28 P.M. *The last segment—and my eyes close on the day.*

MARRIED WITH CHILDREN: A DAY IN THE LIFE OF THE FEMALE ADMINISTRATOR

5:30 A.M.   *The alarm goes off . . . (not music—I might sleep through that, and I can't afford to get up 10 minutes late).*

5:40 A.M.   *Between rolling hair in steam rollers, I drop a load of clothes in the washer. Thank goodness for the automatic coffee maker. My first cup of coffee of the day; nice and strong.*

6:00 A.M.   *While enjoying the coffee, I jot a quick list for the housekeeper . . . especially since the boys had their friends over Saturday night.*

6:05 A.M.   *I rifle through the two reports that were due this morning and the follow-up summary on the conference. We were away this weekend so I couldn't do it earlier. I scan the agenda I needed to write for this afternoon's staff meeting.*

6:15 A.M.   *My navy blue suit, pin-striped shirt, and soft print scarf would be appropriate for the meeting. My favorite blue pearl earrings add a nice touch. A third matching larger blue pearl will hold the scarf in place.*

6:30 A.M.   *While massaging my wedding band I make a pot of decaf for Norm. Thank goodness the children are now old enough to make their own lunches. Times are getting easier. It is nice to have this peace and quiet where I can think about the day ahead. This was my time. The only time I have to plan and reflect.*

6:45 A.M.   *Make-up in place, shoes on, purse and briefcase in hand, I close the front door behind me, knowing Norm will be getting up at any moment. My job takes me further in mileage each day than his. I only have to car pool the kids twice this week.*

7:00 A.M.   *I listened to the notes made this weekend during the conference breaks; I then revised my thoughts for the next workshop. A musical beep told me that one of my associates was calling me—not sure of my location; I grabbed the phone letting her know that I could not work out at my gym tonight; she could still use it and I would meet her tomorrow night after my son's basketball game. Tonight I had to give a talk at the city's Chamber of Commerce. I attempt to work out four times a week, but sometimes it is more difficult; and it has to take last priority behind all of the other demands in my life. My life is full of choices, and each day, each week, each month, and each year I have to sit down and create my goals, objectives and tasks; analyze, prioritize and organize them in perspective.*

This is what it is all about—setting priorities and making time commitments. There is never enough time for everything, so my personal interests are often placed on the back burner. Along the way I have had to make choices based upon my family. I have learned to concentrate and follow through as effectively and efficiently as possible.

My skills and talents have made me a respected leader in the community. I do my job well. I chose a career for which I had educated myself. Twelve years and two babies, three degrees, and two credentials later, I am attempting to balance my personal and professional life. That is the bottom line. It is a game—not always played to the beat of a normal drummer, and never ending. It was all about choices. At the same time I have had to teach everyone in my life to be responsible. They all resisted. It took time, discussions, cajoling, pleading, many fights, and often tears. It could not always be on me. My life had to be organized to the tenth degree in order to make it work.

Lots of guilt. I often feel guilty not having the time or taking the time to spend with my family. Sometimes I wondered why I was doing all this. It seemed like I had forgotten what it was all about. What sacrifices! Often I felt like a stranger to my children. And to Norm. But then I would remember the promise I'd made in college. I would never be dependent on someone to support me. And then later on there was our goal of having a larger home. And college for Danny and Stephen. There was always something.

My job has pressures all of its own. There is much competition in the job market—only the best survive. Not only did I have to compete, but I have to work twice as hard to demonstrate my capabilities to the white males and then be able to stay on top. And then there were often times the lack of support from other women—and the undercurrents of resentment. To be there and to be on top was a lot of work. But work was my middle name.

Oh great! The light's red. I adjust my mascara (I hope Harry is not peeking out of the showroom window. Sam gives me a smile while washing another car.) Two more phone calls and I'm ready for a full day's work.

8:00 A.M.   *The report's given to my secretary; revisions made; the agenda made for the afternoon's meeting; the order is placed for the next semester's textbooks; the conference summary is revised.*

11:45 A.M. Lunch with a city supervisor.

1:00 P.M. Faculty meeting; pre-evaluation conference with an associate professor; advisory session with students.

3:30 P.M. Taught class: Women in Management—Leadership Styles.

5:35 P.M. Going to the City Chamber of Commerce meeting meant less traffic. I thought about my presentation to the Chamber; I needed their support for my next project; that meant I had to sit through another meal of pasta or lasagne. I preferred lighter meals.

6:10 P.M. A quick stop at the grocery store to pick up cold meats, fruit and cookies for the week's lunches. And the drug store to fill a prescription.

6:45 P.M. To the Chamber meeting. Then, finally home.

9:00 P.M. I kick off my heels, peel off my stockings, change to a sweat suit. I join Norm and the boys downstairs. Glancing over Danny's shoulder, I notice Norm smiling at me. I wink back. Thank goodness, I have his support. He is always there in an emergency or a crisis. It seems like everything is an emergency or a crisis. What would I do if I were a single mom!

9:30 P.M. I make a draft of the department budget for this coming semester. There just isn't enough time in the day. But at least I will have a head start on tomorrow's work. This is going to be a productive week. And this coming weekend was something to look forward to. On Saturday we are all going to the football game with dinner in the city afterwards. Sunday, there is the company picnic. A tradition. A family event.

10:15 P.M. I stifle a yawn. A warm shower will feel wonderful. I peeked into the kitchen. All the remains of the bar-be-que were cleaned up. The only indication is the sticky rack left soaking in the sink. There was always something to do. I'll deal with this tomorrow morning when I am not so exhausted. Instead I pick up the children's homework lying on the counter to be proofread.

I guess the biggest frustration of all is that I am always expected to deliver—to be ALL to everyone—my boss, my kids, my husband. Well, I made my choices. No one said it was going to be easy. But I have had to make a balance in my life. A piece of me here, and a piece of me there. I know I am appreciated . . . I am respected. But it wasn't easy. I had to earn it.

These scripts are merely vignettes in the lives of thousands of working women. The success of these women in all areas of their lives depends on careful analysis and planning. Until now, very little has been written about how women can conquer the conflicting issues that confront them in their personal and professional arenas. Imitating the management style of their fathers, husbands, and brothers has proved unsatisfactory. Since women are emerging in our society as independent, clear-thinking, energetic beings, they need to assume an appropriate management style that reflects their new roles.

Respect for a woman's intellect along with high-powered leadership skills is often difficult to sell especially when it comes in an attractive package. The old stereotypes, the judgments, the misinterpretations, the discriminations must be put aside. There is still a great deal of unwillingness to confront blatant issues such as the emergence of the effective woman manager/administrator. There is continual denial regarding sexism not only in our society but throughout all of our institutions.

Respect needs to be earned. The knowledge that women are different from men—not only physiologically, but in the way they think, act, and communicate—needs to be noted, learned, and appreciated. The management community is now taking a closer and more thorough look at what makes an effective leader. We see leadership style becoming a blend of both male and female behavioral traits, with women's socialization skills and abilities being valued.[1]

As the literature suggests, androgyny describes this new management mode. Psychologically, androgyny suggests that "it is possible for people to exhibit both masculine and feminine qualities and that such values, attitudes, and behaviors reside in varying degrees in each of us." [2] Not only are the roles of the sexes changing both physically and professionally, but organizations are analyzing, critiquing, and evaluating the issues that underlie the white male-dominated management arena and the emergencies of the female behavioral traits as they affect issues in management.

The woman administrator of the 21st Century needs to understand these issues and how they affect both her personal and professional growth. Standards for successful organizations—businesses, politics, and education—all need to have a better understanding of male-female relationships. This is a challenging opportunity for management "to develop a style that could increase both employee and organizational effectiveness."[3]

The impact on the organization will not only be felt globally, but also individually. Men and women will be taking a conscious look at themselves in defining "their own behavior and interpreting that of others." Discomfort may set in as with any social change. "People will be practicing behavior foreign to their early teaching and ongoing socialization, and they will have problems readily accepting unaccus-tomed behavior in others."[4]

Androgyny to women in administrative positions renders a con-scious duplicity between their feminine socialization and the perceived male behavioral traits required of managers. We have a tendency to define particular characteristics as being female versus male. "An-drogyny, if adapted by men and women as the most effective man-agement strategy, may help resolve" this dilemma.[5]

Resolution will have to be acclaimed globally by both men and women. Overall, research substantiates that women are perceived to have far fewer management characteristics than men. Both genders credit successful managers "in general to possess characteristics, attitudes, and temperaments ascribed more commonly to men than to women."[6]

These masculine characteristics include leadership ability, com-petitiveness, self-confidence, objectivity, aggressiveness, forcefulness, decisiveness, ambitiousness, and the desire for responsibility. Femi-nine attributes associated with management are understanding, cre-ativity, intuition, and the ability to integrate feelings with thought and behavior.

Women who perceived themselves as effective administrators align themselves with both feminine and masculine behavioral character-istics. They have the best of both worlds. Those women who over-indulge into the male manager image syndrome find themselves in a quandary. No one may appreciate their "enlightened" position.

Androgyny in the administrative work place demonstrates the "value of masculine and feminine traits working in tandem. Charac-teristics from both ends of the sex-role spectrum will become respected management capacities. Women will no longer find it necessary to disassociate their 'feminine' behaviors as they acquire characteristics more typical of men."[7] A successful administrator for the 21st Century will have particular management behavioral traits regardless of the gender.

While affirmative action and equal opportunity programs have opened the doors for women both professionally and personally, simply promoting women to positions of leadership is not the answer.[8] Women must have the ability.

PROFILE FOR SUCCESS

The successful woman administrator creates a blueprint for per-sonal ownership and professional growth. She is the architect of her future, creating all the changes, building upon personal beliefs and prior experiences; shaping her life by purposes and principles—all a part of

the vision that is nothing less than reaching for the stars. The necessary ingredients include:
- personal/professional expectations
- ongoing challenging tasks
- individuals who provide support in accomplishing the tasks.

Overall, the vision:
- creates and communicates a picture
- guides and unifies actions
- aids efficiency and lessens frustrations
- induces commitment toward a mission.[9]

The successful woman administrator is in charge of all the pieces of the vision she designs and creates. Creating a vision is a major responsibility and must take into account the challenges that await, for successfully mastering challenges are the prescription for success. Specific strategies must be practiced to attain the vision.[10] The literature suggests "that people are willing to make a significant investment of time, talent and energy in exchange for enhancement and fulfillment of these three needs:"
- find their work and personal lives meaningful, purposeful, sensible and significant; with a balance maintained between work and play;
- have some reasonable control and influence over their work activities and circumstances;
- experience success, think of themselves as winners, and receive recognition for their efforts.[11]

To handle administrative positions, women need the opportunity to demonstrate their capabilities, and need encouragement to succeed through education, experience, and positive attitudes.

ISSUES AFFECTING THE WOMAN ADMINISTRATOR

From early childhood women are not raised to be leaders, nor are they conditioned to develop the skills and attitudes that are needed to become effective administrators. Positions of leadership have been created by men. "The very culture of business is male, born of a mindset that views competition, gamesmanship, and control as virtues (and traditionally feminine qualities as signs of weakness)."[12]

Social programming and the effects of sexism will not disappear overnight, but women who choose to succeed will see it as a challenge and will use it to their advantage. By learning the rules of competition and assertion, women become more determined than ever to succeed in a male-dominated culture.

What are the issues facing women administrators? How should they be handled? What are the prescriptions for making the road of effective management/administration more easily attainable?

Skill Building

Social conditioning from childhood taught the male how to compete and how to win—a step in the social programming of learning. The rules of competition and assertion promote self-confidence and self-esteem. There were no guidelines, no stepping stones for women growing up. Girls were not taught to be leaders. Confidence was not programmed into girls. They were not taught to take risks.

Women who realize that they lack the social "male" programming from childhood are now planning their careers in leadership positions early on. They have made great strides in obtaining jobs that require post-secondary education and/or skill building. Training in goal-setting and planning, budgeting, decision-making, problem-solving, finance, and other areas are recommended. According to the U.S. Department of Labor as recently as 1989, women's share of management positions reached 45 percent. The executive, administrative, and managerial field will account for 40 percent, or eight million, of the job growth between 1986 and 2000.[13]

Women were not conditioned to be aggressive, but supportive and nurturing. Girls were taught to be compliant and self-effacing. Boys were taught to push forward and make decisions. Failure was not part of their vocabulary. Women may be more "focused on the process, and how to get things done" rather than seeking results."[14] Women need to study the androgynous modes—learn from the male profile yet not lose site of their female roots.

Positive Attitudes

Our white male-dominated society makes those concerned for the competing female in the job market take a look at the barriers both internal and external that can come in the way of professional growth. Internal barriers might be a woman's feeling of inadequacy in a position, low self-image, lack of confidence, or lack of motivation or aspiration. External barriers are not individual but are more global and they require social and institutional reconstruction. An example is sex discrimination. Only time and the pressures of change will eliminate them.

The following positive attitudinal developments will help overcome internal barriers:

- individual self-awareness and a positive self-image
- confidence in her abilities and the ability to inspire, encourage, motivate, and promote others
- an assertive posture appropriate to goal-setting (i.e., viewing the glass half full not half empty)
- assumption of leadership roles, including career commitment, vision, and flexibility.[15]

As the female administrator cultivates and earns respect, she will gain confidence as a role model to others.[16] This is a validation of her success.

Mentoring

There is no substitute for having an experienced, respected individual watching over you, pushing you in the right direction, giving you advice and introducing you to the right people. There is a desperate need for positive reinforcement and constructive criticism. Everyone needs it. A prospective mentor may be a senior individual in management; or an experienced peer. The mentor may be female or male. There may be one, two, or three. However mentoring will be the most successful if the following is adhered to:

- work styles of mentor and protege are similar
- the career advice provided by the mentor is best for you
- the mentor has allegiance to you
- and you do not become dependent on the mentor.[17]

Fortunate is the woman administrator who has this support and is able to reciprocate to others.

Networking

Networking is an informal support system that can be used by women administrators in the development of a career plan. Men have had this system in place for a long time and recognize the importance of this camaraderie tool. Enterprising "career-minded" women will also take advantage of the opportunity to benefit from networking. Recognizing that diversification can lend itself to an enriching balance in her mission to succeed, she will network with both men and women.

To begin networking, women should identify key individuals who can assist them in both the immediate work circle and beyond the organization. Hennig and Jardim suggest "women will have to be willing to set limits on competing among themselves for unrealistic reasons."[18] Career opportunities exist for competent women and support, help, and advice is also available for women who explore this avenue.

Communication

The behavior of an administrator is constantly acknowledged through informal and formal communication, both verbal and non-verbal. Effective administrators recognize how their behavior imparts their goals and objectives, expectations and decisions.

Again, role-modeling is pragmatic. Administrative leaders are observed in everything they do, whether it is the most informal decision or the most calculated.

Dorothy Sarnoff, a communications consultant, works with individuals in improving their methods of communication. Sarnoff's rules for better communication are:

- Do not relax. A little tension can be positive.
- Look from eye to eye. The audience wants to be addressed
- Be animated. Do not just smile.
- Do not fidget. Playing with things does not become the speaker.
- Listen well. Half of all communication is listening.
- Know your audience.
- Dress the role. Women are critiqued more by their appearance than men.
- Develop self-acceptance of your own style—do not be a male clone.
- Learn and be aware of the diversity of other cultures.
- Cultivate your intuitive skills.
- Give a firm, confident handshake. Eye contact is imperative. And smile.[19]

Women administrators who strive to improve their communication abilities can be an asset to any organization.

Sexual Harassment

Sexual harassment comes in many forms: from calling a woman "dear" or "honey," to threatening with demotion, a bad performance evaluation, or being fired if sexual favors are not exchanged. Not only is this unprofessional; it is unlawful. Sometimes the harasser does not even realize what is taking place.

An individual does not have to submit to this unwanted sexual behavior. The best procedure to address the problem is to:

- communicate firmly to the individual regarding the unwanted behavior (it doesn't hurt to be tactful)
- document the behavior if it is repeated
- discuss the situation with another professional
- contact the supervisor or Department Affirmative Action Officer to enter an informal complaint

A woman administrator can assist in preventing the problem of sexual harassment by:

- being businesslike in personal conduct; being a role model for other women
- dressing appropriately for the position
- speaking up if harassment is suspected
- discussing harassment with employees
- being diplomatic and direct.[20]

Women often experience, but deny, sexual harassment. As a survival mechanism women may be inclined to ignore it, play it off, or avoid it. By acknowledging that harassment has occurred, the woman would have to confront it directly, and it might affect her career. Respect needs to be maintained between all employees of both sexes at every level, for there is no place for sex discrimination or sexual irresponsibility in the workplace.

Risk-Taking

The ability to take risks is a necessary behavioral trait in effective administrators. A career cannot be built without taking risks. Men perceive risks as opportunities for success; women tend to look at risks with a fear of failure. Risk-taking is a learned behavior. Female children are not taught this behavior—they are raised to be protected. The ability to take risks is acquired through the socialization process, however, "risk consciousness" can be learned:

- plan carefully
- create long-term goals incorporated with the flexibility to change
- be private with your plans. Do not address them commonly to others. They may be given to the wrong people
- control the size of the risks, and the time in between
- be sensitive to the timing factor. When is the best time?
- build a support system; power means to empower others to formulate a collaborative team
- learn to work with personal stress; be in control of your life.[21]

For women, one of the best ways to learn the art of risk-taking is by observing it in others. Find role models in other women. Determine what has made them successful in taking risks. Become aware of the risks of short-term and long-term goals.

Family Responsibilities

The female administrator who has responsibilities outside of her career must balance her work, home, and personal needs. The male administrator looks to his wife, even if she has a career, to raise their children and take care of the home. She is part of his "support team." More and more professional men are taking a role in the raising of the children, and sharing in household tasks, but generally speaking, it is the woman who is the manager of the home.

Fulfillment for both men and women can enhance their self-concept as they expand their contribution to the home and workplace. Men, in performing household tasks, give women more recognition and respect for their role as the "housewife." They also learn independence in taking over home responsibilities. Women, also, are gaining self-esteem and earning admiration as they become empowered in the work force.

But it is still the woman who must be able to correlate the difficult roles in which she participates into a harmonious situation, both in the workplace, and at home. Consequently, expectations placed on a woman can either make a career opportunity more challenging, thus successful, or more stressful, and perhaps debilitating to her health.

CONCLUSION

As women's leadership qualities begin to influence the definition of an effective administrator in the work force, the integration of female values combined with the already established male leadership traits will produce a collaborative union. The androgynous manager will result from this union. The existing stereotype of effective leadership has already been directly affected by the influx of women into various roles in management and administration.

The woman administrator for the 21st Century will be a self-confident visionary with skills that can match any effective leader—male or female. The promotion of effective leadership will only result in a working environment conducive to giving women the opportunity to succeed. Only then will women be able to have it all.

ABSTRACT

Colleges and universities must include in their staff development efforts programs for advancing women into administrative positions. Mentorships must be viewed as a major way to provide a new and fresh group of administrators for the next generation. In addition, course work in doctoral programs that prepare students for higher education administration should include internships where a student is mentored by a successful administrator.

This formalization of mentoring in colleges and universities must be given its real place of importance—it should receive funding like all other forms of faculty development. This means mentoring should be a part of the options available when funds are allocated to faculty development—aside from money for research, professional travel, and teaching effectiveness, mentoring should be considered as a viable option for career advancement.

Sabbaticals and leaves should be used for mentoring activities— and release time during the academic year should be provided for those interested in mentoring. It is time we take a more aggressive posture about the preparation of women for administrative positions in higher education.

Women administrators need to take the leadership in this move to legitimize mentoring because they have the most need and thus the most to gain. More people in power positions should make it their responsibility to locate and prepare the next generation of leaders. Women leaders could set the pace and sponsor this initiative.

Chapter Seven

Women and Mentoring in Higher Education Administration

Fay L. Bower

*M*entoring is a common aspect of every successful administrator's career. Academic administrators have often been mentored and frequently find themselves mentoring others. For women in academic administration in higher education, mentoring is a very important way to "make it" in a world not necessarily familiar or accommodating. In a world predominantly composed of, run by, and culturally designed for men, mentoring for women becomes a requirement rather than a nicety. Men have understood the value of mentoring for some time and because of the many opportunities available to them have advanced to managerial positions with little difficulty. Having a mentor has been linked with faster promotion and higher pay, greater knowledge of both technical and organizational aspects of business, and higher levels of productivity and performance of both mentors and proteges.[1]

Women have been joining the work force in increasing numbers for the last decade and now comprise a substantial percentage of the work force. While this is an important and growing change, another

FAY L. BOWER *is President of Clarkson College in Omaha, Nebraska. Prior to that, she worked as Director of University Planning and Institutional Research at the University of San Francisco. She has also served as Interim Vice-President, Academic Affairs and Dean of the School of Nursing at the University of San Francisco. Dr. Bower has published widely in the field of nursing. She has served on many professional boards as well as chair of many professional committees. She holds a B.S. from San Jose State College, M.S.N. from the University of California at San Francisco, and D.N.Sc. from the University of California at San Francisco.*

important fact is that the majority of these women work at lower level jobs. This is true in the public sector as well as in agencies and businesses in the private sector.

There are many factors that influence women's career decisions. Social images and American values are often contradictory in terms of women and work. Ambivalence and ambiguity about career choices and measures of success tend to be present more often with women than men. In a search for answers as to why women remain at lower or mid-level jobs, sex role stereotyping is the reason most often proposed.[2] While stereotyping certainly contributes to women's lack of progress upward, stereotypical attitudes neither individually nor collectively account for differences in career development.

There has also been much debate over whether differences in ability exist between men and women and if they exist, whether they influence managerial potential. While this debate will probably continue for some time, research tends to refute the idea and supports the notion that there are no significant differences between women and men that would limit a woman's ability to function as a manager or supervisor.[3]

Another factor that has contributed to keeping women at lower level jobs is the long-term socialization process that influences role development. A part of this process is the mentoring relationship whereby an experienced person provides guidance and support to the developing novice. Women have had limited access to this kind of relationship and consequently suffer a significant disadvantage in competing with their male counterparts for promotion and advancement. Williams and Blackburn suggest that a direct working relationship is most beneficial in the development of the protege.[4]

There have been few studies on the impact of a mentoring relationship or lack of mentoring in the career development of women. Most notable is the work of Henning and Jardim in which they identified the following characteristics of high level female executives:

1. Their mothers were "caregivers" rather than career women.
2. Early identification was with the father rather than mother.
3. The father-daughter relationship was very special. Femininity was not rejected nor were they treated like boys. Unlike the son, the daughter was never a rival nor did she have to compete with the mother for the father's attention.
4. They delayed motherhood in favor of a career, and most remained with the same firm until they got a high level position.
5. Their mentor was their boss who in effect took over the father's role.
6. They remained dependent on their mentors until they reached mid-management.[5]

Sheehy has written about mentor relationships and their impact on women's careers and she came to similar conclusions. Women who had gained recognition in their careers had had mentor relationships even if they did not recognize them as such.[6]

If mentor relationships are so vital to career development for women administrators, what are the reasons women do not form such relationships? The following reasons are suggested by the literature:

1. The absence of women role models has an inhibiting effect on the career advancement of women. Women do not advance because they lack reliable insights successful businesswomen could give them.[7]

2. Mentor relationships are an aspect of social learning that is the result of mixing and relating. Women as youngsters often do not participate in team sports to the extent that men do. Thus men are more likely to develop the skills necessary for a mentoring relationship and as a result take them into the working environment.[8]

3. Women rarely provide a mentor relationship. This is commonly known as the "queen bee" phenomena which suggests there is only room for one outstanding woman in an organization and that each other woman must fight her way to the top just as the "queen bee" did.

4. There are potential sexual aspects of the male-female relationship that keep men from becoming mentors to aspiring women. For fear of having his motives misunderstood by his peers or because the interest is already present, the would-be mentor stays detached and uninvolved with the talented women.

5. Another reason men do not become mentors to women is because they do not perceive talent that merits attention. Many successful men do not consider women to be serious about careers. Epstein calls this the pattern of revocability. "American women have cultural approval to 'cop out.' Those women who choose to leave an occupation or profession at any level, from training to practice, do so with society's full approval and will be given credit for having reached whatever level they have attained, though a man in a similar situation would be considered a failure."[9]

CHALLENGES FOR WOMEN IN HIGHER EDUCATION

At most colleges and universities, many persons in key decision-making positions—deans, vice presidents, and presidents—have achieved those positions largely because someone older, wiser, and more powerful saw in them indications of leadership potential and encouraged them to develop that potential. Mentors often are important in the development of successful college administrators. Levinson's work on the life course of adult men, underscores the critical role played by an older man who decides to use his experiences and position to help a young protege, and Kanter speaks of "young executives who receive a boost into the fast lane through direct help from a senior colleague."[10] Mentoring is not only important at the personal level but also at the institutional level. While the protege may look upon the mentor as a career enhancer, institutions like colleges ought to regard the mentor as a valuable talent scout and trainer.

For women in higher education mentoring presents some unique challenges. Along with those already discussed, mentoring in a college or university is complicated by the fact that administrators rise from the faculty ranks, a position totally different from the one they seek, and that they have been judged and reinforced for their faculty skills by their peers not their superiors. During the peer review process faculty learn to judge one another on their ability to teach and do research, not on their ability to manage or administer. So the rewards are not those that would foster the development and improvement of management skills. Unless an administrator recognizes the faculty person's potential for administration and mentors that person, it is unlikely the person will advance into administration.

For men, this advancement in higher education has not been too difficult. A look at who holds the president, vice president, dean, chair and director positions in colleges and universities validates this point. It is here that the issues cited earlier are evident. Since there are few women in administrative positions who can act as mentors, there are limited same-sex mentors. Most women administrators in higher education positions today cite men as their mentors and since there is the fear by men of sexual involvement (or the perception of such) few men want to mentor women.

There is another problem confronting women in higher education. Because groups in which most of the members share a common bond are not likely to accept persons who do not share the similarities, women in higher education find it difficult when they are selected as proteges into all male groups. Once selected they may be subjected to additional stresses. Because the woman is frequently the only woman in an all men inner circle, she may become tagged as the token woman. The sense of specialness, of being exceptional, may also cause her to keep other women out of the group. Moreover, the additional performance demands of being "the only one" often keep them from functioning as mentors themselves.[11]

Women in higher education administrative positions today, unlike their forerunners, are often married and mothers. These additional responsibilities create other burdens for advancement. Conflicts about priorities often place the woman in a stressful position. Balancing the demands of higher education administration with the responsibilities of a parent and a spouse is not easy. Hardly a day goes by without an article in the media about the stresses on marriage and parenting and how to cope with them when a career is pursued.

Another more subtle challenge is the development of a career as an administrator in a male-dominated environment while still maintaining an identity as a woman. In the '70s there were a plethora of articles in the lay literature on how to dress for success. The proposals presented were so reflective of male dress—black tailored suit, briefcase to replace the purse and no four-inch spiked heels. "Frill and fluff" were discouraged, as were bright makeup and dangling earrings. The message was clear; to succeed in a career the model was a male one. Over the last 20 years the advice has been much more realistic but the problem of "making it" in a male dominant career is still a matter of finding a fit without discarding self. Having a woman mentor who has been able to master this conflict is an important aspect of a woman's success in a career predominantly male filled.

THE DEMANDS ON WOMEN IN HIGHER EDUCATION

The demands on women in higher education administration are twofold: Women need to learn their roles and be as good as men in a world fairly foreign to them. A good example of this dilemma was shared by Sara Weddington—the lawyer who won the 1972 *Roe vs Wade* case—in a speech she gave in Nashville, Tennessee at the National League for Nursing's biennial convention in June, 1991. She once worked in Jimmy Carter's administration as his assistant and was assigned to explore women's issues. She told about her experiences as a decision maker among men decision makers in the federal government. She told about discovering that her decisions were different than her male colleagues' because they were based on a different premise and the wrong outcome. While her colleagues were playing golf with important constituents, she was diligently answering her mail, believing it important to respond individually to each letter and wanting to "get it all cleaned up." While this was important, she was missing a critical opportunity to learn the informal news and to develop a network of peers for support. It was a world foreign to her and there was no one around to teach her the "tricks of the trade."

This same experience, while a little different, faces women administrators in higher education. For all the reasons discussed earlier, women have few woman role models and when they are mentored by men they often get into conflict with what is expected and their own values and work styles.

Finding a role model who will mentor, even in a world where women are plentiful, is not an easy task. As Kanter has pointed out, competence or high-level performance is usually not sufficient to gain power or the attention of the powerful.[12] An aspiring administrator in academe has "to contribute something important to the organization beyond her or his normal job responsibilities, something that may involve risk and increase visibility. It might be accidental, coincidental, or planned, but it must be authentic, that is, it must be part of the institution's regular activities."[13] This is usually the first step in the formation of a mentor-protege relationship. Furthermore, it most often is the mentor who recognizes the talented protege.

MENTORING IN HIGHER EDUCATION ADMINISTRATION

Most of the mentoring in higher education is of the tutelage kind. The selection is specific; a dean, vice president, or president selects a faculty person to do a specific task because it is believed the faculty person has a special talent. Additional tests may be constructed by the mentor that arise naturally from the responsibilities assigned. The protege may even feel there is a "watch" time, a time for the protege to prove him or her self. However, this phase doesn't last long because most mentors in higher education see themselves as reasonably good judges of character and talent.[14] Another way the selection takes place is by committee assignment. In this way proteges can be spotted and nourished by an administrator.

Once the administrator is comfortable with the selection of a protege the relationship moves to another plane. The protege is chosen to work closely with the mentor, to accept a lesser role than the mentor's, but one that requires close, often daily contact. The new appointment has the effect of moving the protege into the inner circle not as a full-fledged member but under the protection of the mentor.

The goal of the protege in the mentor relationship is both one of doing well and being developed. The protege is given an opportunity to see the college or university from a different perspective and is provided with a chance to contribute in a different way and with a higher impact. The protege gets to see the "bigger picture," to have access to special, privileged, and even secret information and is taken into the confidence of those in the "inner circle" and so becomes accepted by them.

An important aspect of the protege-mentor experience is the impact it can have on the mentor and the institution. Proteges get things done; they learn and develop while they do work for the mentor, thus gaining experience while helping the mentor meet his or her goals for the institution.

Developing a protege in higher education takes many forms. Proteges learn incidental things—how to dress and travel—and important things, like the politics of the institution and the issues faced by the institution at the local, state, and federal level. They learn how to relate with people, especially difficult ones, how to listen, what battles to take on, what issues to avoid, and above all how to judge a situation. Most proteges learn to look at situations as their mentors did, often asking of themselves, how would he or she (the mentor) assess this situation?

Probably the most important benefit of the mentor-protege relationship is its power for career advancement of the protege. Some mentors are specific and open about their intentions. They select a protege for a specific position. The protege knows he or she is being groomed for the deanship or vice presidency, for instance. Other mentors leave the options open making it clear the goal is to develop competence and contacts.

Developing connections is a major outcome of the mentor-protege relationship. Research has identified the value of colleague relations for lawyers, physicians, and academicians. Sharing interests, performance, and contributions, proteges are able to extend their sphere of impact and their options for future advancement. Mentors introduce their proteges to the inner circle of administrators beyond the walls of the institution thus providing a variety of possibilities. Such colleague systems are the means by which the protege gains influence and power. The promise of contacts through the mentor is often crucial for the protege and helps diffuse some of the emotional tension of the relationship, specifically, the tension of taking the next step—to succeed the mentor. As Levinson pointed out, there are several functions mentors must perform: teacher, sponsor, guidance counselor, exemplar role model, and initiator while providing moral support and an indoctrination into the values and ways of the position pursued.[15] Essentially it is a transition from the parent-child relationship to an adult-peer relationship. So ultimately the mentor relationship is for the mentor to help the protege develop to a position of equality and be prepared for a similar position or one of higher magnitude. Colleague connections can take the protege beyond the mentor, doing it in such a way that provides the mentor with pride in the protege's accomplishments.

CONCLUSION

While there are an increasing number of women administrators in higher education today, there is a need for those women to avoid the "queen bee" trap and to actively promote and provide mentoring of younger, less experienced women. Formal programs need to be established where women higher education administrators can meet and mentor women who are interested in administrative positions. We can no longer expect mentoring to happen, because it doesn't occur at the rate necessary to make up the inequity in higher education. We need more structured and deliberate action.

ABSTRACT

It has long been known that environmental and social factors play significant roles as motivators of individual achievement. While much has been written about what motivates men to achieve, a profile of women of achievement and the factors that motivate them only began to emerge in the literature as late as the 1960s. Even then, no distinction was made between what motivates Black women to achieve and what motivates White women.

The authors of this chapter conducted their own survey of Black women and White women of achievement—focusing on social, historical, and cultural factors that may be similar or unique to both populations. The following chapter sheds new light on the differences and the similarities between these two populations of women.

Chapter Eight

Environmental and Social Factors in the Respective Backgrounds of Black Women and White Women of Achievement

Joyce Owens and Patricia Turner Mitchell

*T*he motivation to achieve has been described as a motive to be competent in a situation in which there are standards of excellence and where there is risk involved. Individuals who have such motivation are attributed such qualities as independence, persistence, and the ability to undertake realistic tasks; they have internal standards of excellence, a clear understanding of their goals, and they perform well academically.[1]

JOYCE OWENS is currently working with the Economic Opportunity Prevention Services Program at San Francisco City College. Dr. Owens worked with the Women's Center also for several years. She is a Licensed Clinical Social Worker who has conducted extensive research in the area of psychology of women and gender issues. She received her B.A. from San Francisco State, M.S. from the University of California at Berkeley, and her Ed.D. from the University of San Francisco.

PATRICIA MITCHELL is a faculty member in the School of Education at the University of San Francisco. Dr. Mitchell earned her Ph.D. in Educational Administration and Higher Education from The Catholic University of America in Washington, D.C.

Early studies of motivation in achieving males abound in the literature. Results of these studies indicated that male achievers were not necessarily motivated by status. They were motivated by challenges that created a moderate degree of uncertainty. They also tended to expect success and to be bored with routine and mechanical activities. Taylor, in a review of the literature about underachievers, found seven major differences between achieving and underachieving students without taking into account sex differences. His conclusions regarding distinctions between achievers and non-achievers are provocative: in contrast to nonachievers, achievers are task-oriented, self-confident, independent, structured, and less social. In addition, their goals are realistic and they generally have a seriousness of purpose.[2]

Although research has thus described the attributes of achieving individuals in general, it tells us little about achieving women in particular and reveals nothing about the role of race and culture as it influences women of achievement.[3] The need to clarify the motivation to achieve among women is underscored by the profound changes in the roles of women during the past century.[4] Equally profound changes in the roles and status of Blacks and Black females in particular pose a similar need for clarification of their motives for achievement. Changes in the status of Blacks following the Civil Rights Movement, as well as changes induced by factors affecting the status of all women, encouraged women of varying backgrounds, ages, and cultures to swell the ranks of America's work force. With the educational achievement of women rising dramatically and the awareness by industry of the growing numbers of qualified women, researchers predict that women in the 1990s will enter a greater variety of occupational areas in ever-increasing numbers. Consequently, achievement as it specifically relates to women has become a subject of serious interest to researchers and historians.[5]

A profile of the achieving woman and the factors that motivate her began to emerge in the 1960s and continues to be delineated in the literature. At the same time, it has become increasingly apparent to a number of Black researchers that findings applicable to White populations of women do not apply to Black populations. In light of the research cited, studies of Black women in a cultural and historical context require serious consideration and must be placed within an historical framework which is carefully researched, documented, and reinterpreted.[6]

A number of White researchers became aware of the inconsistencies in their research when findings that were true of White populations were applied to Black populations. The results of these studies substantiated the growing concern of Black researchers about the application of research results for White populations and the extent to which these findings could be generalized to Black populations.[7]

Early studies on achievement motivation in women indicated that the individuals most likely to succeed often did not fulfill their full potential. According to Horner, many young women who reveal a need to avoid success are, paradoxically, those whose potential for achievement is high. Fear of success, or the motive to avoid success, as described by Horner includes anticipation of negative consequences because of success, a direct or indirect expression of conflict about success, or the denial of effort or responsibility for attaining success.[8]

Women whose high achievement motivation is not undercut by the fear of success are, oppositely, characterized by their anticipation of positive consequences of success, lack of conflict about success, and their willingness to claim responsibility for success.

The authors asked the question, "Are there unique criteria in evaluating support systems for Black achieving women?" What characteristics do Black women and White women of achievement share? Our study focused on social, historical, and cultural factors that may be similar or unique to the Black and White populations of the research.

We asked the following questions:

1. What constitutes the nuclear family for Black women and White women as it may affect their achievement motivation?
2. Is there a difference between Black women and White women in the mean age at which they begin to rear children?
3. How do they perceive the possibility of successfully combining career and family life?
4. What resources are needed and utilized in order to pursue higher degrees?
5. From whom do Black women and White women of achievement seek advice concerning future plans, choice of career, and further training?
6. What roles do they prefer to play in their work situations?
7. Do they see women's roles as determined by society or by individual choice?
8. How do Black women and White women of achievement perceive a desirable male-female relationship?
9. How assertive are they in critical or difficult situations?
10. How do they compare on measures of self-concept?

Research on achievement motivation has historically focused on such factors as the influence of significant others, role models, and environmental and cultural influences. The nature and scope of these findings, however, were limited by the fact that the subjects of these studies were predominantly male.[9] In women, other factors such as the fear of success, the relationship between early marriage and childrearing plans, resources used in the pursuit of higher education, the effect of networks and mentors on achievement, and self concept influence the motivation to achieve.

Consequently, although a general knowledge of factors contributing to achievement motivation has been gained, there is still a need for further research on achievement motivation in women and the relationship between culture and achievement among women.[10]

METHOD

In order to examine this phenomena, a multiple choice questionnaire was devised by the investigators to elicit responses to the research questions regarding the background of Black women and White women of achievement. In addition, the Tennessee Self Concept Scale was administered in order to measure the self concept of the subjects who participated in the study. Each subject was asked to complete both instruments.

Owens Multiple Choice Questionnaire

This instrument was developed by the researchers specifically for this study; it was designed to answer the research questions cited earlier. Its purpose was to obtain specific information about the individual, the individual in relation to her ethnic group, and the group to which she relates.

Tennessee Self Concept Scale

The TSCS consists of 100 self-descriptive statements which the women use to portray their own pictures of themselves. This study employed the clinical and research form which consists of 29 profiled scores.

The sample included 26 Black women and 38 White women of achievement selected from six women's business and professional organizations, three of which have primarily White membership and three of which have primarily Black membership.

RESULTS

The findings of the study are as follows:

Question #1: What constitutes the nuclear family for Black women and White women as it may affect their achievement motivation? Ninety-two percent of the White subjects as compared to 64 percent of the Black subjects defined the nuclear family as consisting only of mother, father, sister, and brother. A significantly higher number of Blacks, (28 percent as compared to only 6 percent of the White subjects) defined the nuclear family as consisting also of other relatives (P < .05).

Question #2: Is there a difference between Black women and White women in the mean age at which they begin to rear children? Five percent (or 2) of the White subjects, as compared to 12 percent (or 3) of the Black subjects first became pregnant between the ages of 12 and 19. Of the White subjects, 34 percent (or 13), as compared to 46 percent (or 12) of the Black subjects, first became pregnant between the ages of 20 and 29. Of the White subjects, 3 percent (or 1) first became pregnant between the ages of 30-35 and 3 percent (or 1) first became pregnant after the age of 36. None of the Black subjects became pregnant after the age of 30.

Question #3: How do Black women and White women of achievement perceive the possibility of successfully combining career and family life?

More Black women (69 percent) than White women (50 percent) believe that it is possible to combine career and family life most of the time, even though this difference was not statistically significant. There were no significant differences between Black and White subjects on their perceptions of whether marital status affects a successful career. In fact, the vast majority of both groups felt that it did not matter whether a woman was single or married.

Both Black women and White women of achievement almost unanimously believe that women seeking a career can combine career and family. Three White subjects indicated that a career should wait until after children are raised; no Black subjects, however, indicated that this was the preferred option for career women.

Question #4: What resources are needed and utilized by Black women and White women of achievement in order to pursue higher degrees? Eighty-seven percent of the White sample and 92 percent of the Black sample completed college or post-baccalaureate degrees. A larger percentage of the Black sample (77 percent as compared to 68 percent of the White sample) had pursued post-graduate education.

An item in the Owen questionnaire asked those subjects who completed college or above if they were funded by grants, parents, self-employment, or other. A significantly higher number of White subjects (79 percent or 33) than Black subjects (50 percent or 12), were funded by their parents in the pursuit of higher education. A significantly higher number of Blacks, 46 percent (or 11) as compared to 14 percent (or 4) Whites were funded by other sources. Of the White subjects, 93 percent (or 27) as compared to 62 percent (or 15) of the Black subjects funded their education through self-employment and 41 percent of the White subjects, (or 12) as compared to 50 percent of the Blacks (or 12) funded their education through receipt of grants.

Among the White subjects, 17 percent were funded by one source; 52 percent were funded by two sources; 28 percent were funded by three sources; and 3 percent were funded by four sources. Among the Black subjects, 33 percent or 8 were funded by one source; 38 percent were funded by two sources; 21 percent were funded by three sources;

and 8 percent were funded by four sources. The findings indicate that there is a higher percentage of White women than Black women who are dependent on multiple sources of funding in the pursuit of education past high school.

Question #5: From whom do Black women and White women of achievement seek advice concerning future plans, choice of career, and further training?

Twenty-four percent of the White women and 19 percent of the Black women seek advice in making plans or choosing a college education. While the majority of both Black women and White women used their own judgment as indicated by 76 percent of the White women and 81 percent of the Black women who responded.

Forty-two percent of all of the women indicated they do not rely on any of the references listed in choosing a career. Of the White women, 32 percent indicated they were influenced by a friend or relative in choosing a career as compared to 31 percent of the Black women who were influenced by a relative and 27 percent of the Black women who indicated they were influenced by a friend. Of the White women, 18 percent, as compared to 15 percent of the Black women, were influenced by others in choosing a career.

A significantly high number of Black women, (60 percent) as compared to White women (23 percent) make decisions about further training after exposure to new ideas. A significant number of White women, (46 percent), as compared to 20 percent of Black women chose trial and error; 16 percent of the White women and 8 percent of the Black women made decisions about further training based on the trusted advice of another.

Most of the subjects stated the way to learn most effectively was with guidance from someone they respected. Of the Black women, 33 percent, as compared to 19 percent of the White women, learned most effectively in a training program, while 22 percent of all the subjects learned most effectively on their own.

Question #6: What roles do Black women and White women of achievement prefer to play in their work situations?

A significant number of Black women, (40 percent as compared to 17 percent of White women), are more comfortable in directing others to do the work. Of the White subjects, 47 percent, (as compared to 20 percent of the Black subjects) are more comfortable in making plans for work to be done. About the same number of Black as White subjects, (36 percent) and (40 percent) prefer to do the actual work.

Question #7: Do Black women and White women of achievement see women's role as determined by society or by individual choice?

A significant percentage of the Black subjects (76 percent as compared to an even 50 percent of the White subjects), felt that roles in our society were predetermined.

Question #8: How do Black women and White women of achievement perceive a desirable male-female relationship?

The findings indicate that all of the Black subjects and 97 percent of the White subjects feel that it is desirable to have relationships in which men and women are equal. None of the subjects feel that it is desirable to have relationships in which the man makes the major decisions or the woman makes the major decisions. Only one of the White subjects was undecided. None of the Black subjects were undecided.

Question #9: How assertive are Black women and White women of achievement in critical or difficult situations?

In a situation where their views would be unpopular, a significantly higher percentage of Black subjects, (46 percent), as compared to 19 percent of the White subjects, would state their views. A significantly higher number of White subjects, (70 percent), than Black subjects, (42 percent), would wait before expressing their views. The rest would seek another opinion.

Question #10: How do Black women and White women of achievement compare on measures of self-concept?

Scores on the Tennessee Self-Concept Scale were not significantly different.

The score, as reported, reflects that Black and White subjects have equal amounts of self-esteem with a total positive mean of 263.2 for White subjects and a total positive mean of 260.2 for Black subjects. Standard deviation for White subjects on the total positive score was 9.5, and for Blacks, the standard deviation on the total positive score was 16.5.

DISCUSSION

The number of similarities among the respective Black and White subjects in the sample is remarkable given their different backgrounds and histories. The differences, in the light of such similarities, are even more noteworthy in that they indicate certain definitive characteristics among Black women and White women which are culturally and historically based.

The responses of Black and White subjects in the sample support the observation that erroneous and inaccurate results are highly probable in research on Black populations which does not consider differences in the kinds of nuclear family and role models available to the Black woman who is motivated to achieve. The finding that 28 percent of the Black subjects, as compared to 6 percent of the White subjects in the study defined the nuclear family in terms of other relatives as well as parents and siblings, would indicate that the nuclear family is defined in broader terms for the Black woman than for the White woman. Research should be sensitive to the relative meaning of nuclear family for Black women and White women.

The findings indicate that White women tend to use more resources in funding their education than do Black women. This trend may imply that increased information about the nature and kinds of funding sources would be helpful to all women who are motivated to achieve and that Black women, in particular, would find such knowledge useful.

Responses indicate that Black women tend to rear children while attempting to establish careers while White women tend to establish their careers before rearing their families. However, the responses to question #3 indicates that both groups equally support the idea of combining a career and family in theory even if they are not, in practice, able to achieve that for themselves.

Similarities in responses by Black and White subjects to research questions 3, 5, 7, 8, and 10 indicate the areas in which they are in agreement. The finding that Black women and White women use the support of role models, mentors, support groups, and training in choosing a career and furthering their education implies that the same training models and support systems can be used in assisting all women who are motivated to achieve. More Black women will respond to training programs. The finding that Black women and White women prefer equal relationships with men, as opposed to relationships where one or the other dominates implies that the model of Black matriarchy popular in some American literature bears serious revamping. The finding that Black women and White women have equally high self-esteem implies that the strengths inherent in both groups of women, as opposed to their limitations, should be emphasized in training and support systems.

The differences between the Black and White subjects in the sample, in light of the similarities, are even more striking: Black women are seriously affected by any changes in funding base and have fewer sources they can rely on in their quest for education. Yet, despite such odds, their motivation to achieve is such that they are more highly represented than White women (92 percent Black as compared to 87 percent White) among those who completed college or post-baccalaureate degrees. They are also more highly represented among the subjects who obtained post-baccalaureate degrees (77 percent Black as compared to 68 percent White). A possible implication of such findings is that education as a means of survival and identification with the Black culture are positive incentives for Black women in their motivation to achieve. The finding that Black women are more comfortable in positions of authority lends strong support to the theory of cultural relevance in self concept in that there appears to be more support among Black women than among White women in their respective backgrounds toward being assertive.

Black subjects as opposed to White subjects perceive greater obstacles in society. This would indicate that, despite their self-confidence, Black women are quite aware that the social and environmental factors which impinge on their lives are affected by racism as well as sexism. Consequently, the reality of their lives is, in some respects, different than the reality of the lives of White women.

The influence of racial and historical background is particularly apparent in the significant (P< .05) number of Black women who chose to take a risk in critical situations as opposed to waiting or seeking another opinion. Black women appear to automatically speak out on controversial issues whereas White women generally take the opposite stance of analyzing the situation and then responding. This is another indication of the way in which Black women and White women are influenced by their respective backgrounds in the decision-making process.

In conclusion, the findings indicate the importance of considering the influence of environmental and social factors in the motivation to achieve among Black women and White women. They also indicate that theories which have been formulated about achieving Black women and White women as regards attitudes toward assertion, eduction, family planning, and self concept need further examination and comparison.

Stereotypes about the matriarchal Black family need serious revision. More information is needed about support systems among Black women of different socioeconomic strata, and more information is needed about factors which affect the self concept and subsequent motivation to achieve in Black women.

ABSTRACT

Young women have experienced a "double bind" regarding success and achievement in American society. On the one hand, they are encouraged to be successful and seek academic excellence and new opportunities. On the other hand, the "old boys' network"—the "traditional" structure of society and academia—has created barriers that often prevent women from advancing into leadership positions.

In this chapter, the author explores some of the androcentric or male-centered thinking that still exists and the hurdles within society and within ourselves that deter women on their paths to leadership positions.

Chapter Nine

Questioning the System:
A Feminist Perspective

Mary T. Flynn

During the academic years of 1990 and 1991, I had the opportunity to speak with 15 female chief executive officers who administered public universities throughout the United States. Two consecutive telephone interviews, each of which lasted an average of 35 minutes, were held to discuss what barriers these leaders thought existed within higher education that kept women from aspiring to positions of leadership. What transpired during those conversations is documented here.

HURDLES WITHIN THE ACADEMY

Reserved for White Men

Boards of trustees and regents who make the decisions on hiring at the chancellor/president level are dominated by white males. A lot of "old fashioned sexism" exists in higher education. While women have for a very long time served in various administrative posts, there haven't been very many and never in posts of great decision making. These positions are reserved for white men.

MARY T. FLYNN is currently a faculty member in the psychology department at the University of Wisconsin-Stout. She received her B.A. in psychology from the University of Wisconsin-Eau Claire, M.S.E. in Counseling Psychology from the University of Wisconsin-River Falls, and Ed.D. in Educational Leadership from the University of St. Thomas. Dr. Flynn has conducted research in the area of gender issues and leadership development.

Boards are not comfortable having women fill leadership positions perhaps because of a prevailing belief that men prefer to work with other men. At some point, qualified women are removed from the list of potential applicants thus ensuring a pool consisting only of men—reducing the potential of a viable female candidate being selected.

Some of the institutions that have the opportunity to recruit women as presidents have a great fear that if they do, the institution will not be taken seriously. The major concerns of public institutions are often community relations and fund raising, and it is more comfortable for the institution if the person who has influence over these areas is a man. Reasons cited for removing qualified women from the applicant pool included a belief that women cannot effectively fund raise, will not be taken seriously by the higher education community, and cannot administrate large institutions or competitive sports programs. Vestiges of sexism still exist on the part of boards of trustees and regents who make the decisions about hiring. There is still the belief that women can't raise money and certainly can't administrate over a major football or basketball team.

This androcentric or male-centered thinking is well conceptualized in Anne Wilson Schaef's explanation of how men see relationships in the world. According to Schaef, the "White Male System" is the only thing that exists. This myth implies that the white male view of the world is the right way to understand it, or the only reality. When women attempt to become part of this system, they are told they don't understand reality.[1]

The "White Male System" is innately superior. Innate superiority and innate inferiority are birthrights which cannot be earned or traded away. The "White Male System" knows and understands everything. This is one reason why women so frequently look to men for advice and direction. Both sexes genuinely believe that men should and do know it all. The "White Male System" knows it is possible to be totally logical, rational, and objective. Members of the system spend a lot of time and energy telling women that females are by nature not logical, rational, or objective. As a result white males severely limit women's ability to take in new information and have new experiences.

All too often, male relationships are conceived as being either one-up or one-down. When two people come together or encounter each other, the assumption is that one of them must be superior and the other must be inferior. Those interviewed insisted we need to address these myths and dispel them.

Traditional Structure

In some cases men do not want higher education administration opening up to women because of the change this would require in the social and intellectual structure of the role of chancellor or president.

Boards of trustees that are dominated by white males who are more than fifty years old, envision their presidents with a spouse who serves as the first lady and hostess.

According to the data, the ideal presidential presence includes a spouse—a nonworking female spouse who does not have a separate career from that of her husband. In this society a woman's status is still mainly defined through her husband. If women were to take on more visible positions in administration the leadership image could not remain that of the strong charismatic male with his first lady at his side to serve as the gracious hostess.

This ideal arrangement does not hold true when a woman is the president and her husband plays the role of host. One female chancellor told of how a woman walked up to her at an elegant party the chancellor was hosting and abruptly stated, "I'm certainly glad I don't have to live like you." Women's status is still gained mainly through men so we haven't learned to trust other women. It goes back to the insecurity women feel in the realization that we are expected by societal norms to compete against each other for men. The lack of trust by women of women in leadership roles supports this thinking. Some of the worst detractors can be women. A female chancellor with a husband is an anomaly. One without a husband can be seen as a threat.

Old Boys Network

There are not enough successful men willing to open doors for competent females, thus women miss out on high level positions because they are not part of the traditional "old boys network" which recommends most of the people for top positions.

Mentoring for leadership is still reserved by men for men to a large extent. This is an informal process in which senior executives identify subordinates with potential to assume future leadership roles. These candidates are groomed by executives receiving personal attention and increased involvement at the senior management level. Fierman, in an article published in *Fortune Magazine*, reported this grooming is often conducted in a social framework outside the workplace—on the golf course, over drinks and dinner, or at the gym.[2] This opportunity to explore personal and professional philosophy is important to creating the "fit" necessary for successful management teams. However, the nature of the relationships precludes women. Many business leaders are men socialized in the 1950s who chose future leaders from their own ranks. Because of this men are chosen to be mentored.

Another more subtle problem with including women in the mentoring process is the difficulty of developing professional relationships due to past socialization and sex role stereotyping. Often men view women as mothers, wives, or daughters, and women have been trained to see themselves in these supporting roles. "Women will not be comfortable as leaders as long as they and the men around them perceive their sexual roles as primary."[3] Removing the stereotype is essential if women are to be mentored.

Women are excluded from the informal networks that provide the best leaders to senior positions in higher education.[4] When two individuals are competing for an administrative position the sponsored individual will get the position, even if the other individual has better qualifications. This kind of activity reinforces the replication formula by which white males choose and promote individuals with the same background as their own.[5]

Decision makers surround themselves with leaders who are like themselves because changes in political, legislative, and economic conditions require most institutions of higher education to operate in an environment of uncertainty. When the external environment is uncertain, internal predictability takes on greater importance. For this reason, people in positions of power within higher education are likely to maintain the status quo. This means white males predominate in the highest levels of leadership.[6]

Young women have experienced a "double bind" regarding success and achievement in American society. This results from the mixed messages women have been given during the last 50 years. Our society encourages women through education and opening doors to new opportunity, but at the same time undermines women's self-confidence by creating barriers to leadership positions. Despite admirable academic records and excellent prospects for the future women have been deeply affected by the resistance or resentment they have encountered and by the negative consequences they have learned to anticipate in the professional arena.[7]

Women are assumed to be submissive, dependent, conforming, affectionate, and sympathetic by both males and females. When these beliefs are carried into decision making or used to define professional status for executives or administrators, they foster results likely to place lesser value on female ability. These biased perceptions of women are often identified as the cause for underrepresentation of women in leadership roles.[8] When females are in leadership roles they are judged more harshly by men and women.

Kanter points out that when females reach positions of greater visibility, they become the token women, the topic of gossip and careful scrutiny.[9] Their mistakes and ultimate relationships become common knowledge. They are used as showpieces and held up as an example of how a woman in an administrative position should or should not behave.

HURDLES WITHIN SOCIETY

Social Pressure

There has always been great social pressure on women to marry and have children. Society has always seen this as the female's primary role. During the 19th century, married women didn't teach. If a woman married, she had to quit teaching. This is where the stereotype came from of the old maid school teacher. A lot of women who did get married kept it a secret because they wanted to keep their jobs. There are many options for women today but they take time and the very traditional duties of home and child care are still there. Professional women who are trying to do it all are realizing that the time and focus required of executive officers is so extreme that they are not willing even to commit to the time needed to compete.

A chancellor remembered a dean coming to her for advice because one of his assistant professors was pregnant and intended to teach until the time the baby was born. The chancellor's retort was, "Well she is just pregnant, she's not incapacitated, it hasn't affected her brain."

Submissive stereotypes imposed by society have also made it difficult for women to see themselves in leadership roles. The notion of a leader is someone tough or macho, with an aura of charisma. A role which women don't fit. According to society, women are nurturers and best suited for motherhood and the supportive role of wife.

There is a tendency for both sexes to make negative comments about women who do take on leadership roles. The more important the woman's title, the more controversial her position. Some female administrators find that male colleagues or students routinely address them as "honey" or "dear." It is common for male colleagues to be called "Dr." while females may be addressed as "Mrs." or "Ms." or by their first names. At department meetings they may be expected to record minutes. Their personal lives are often scrutinized. "Who takes care of her kids?" and their appearance commented on, "With legs like those, why don't you wear skirts more often?" Most frustrating of all, their work may be devalued even when it is equal or superior to that of a man. Discrimination like this keeps women out of academe or prevents those already there from moving up.[10]

HURDLES WITHIN OURSELVES

In general, women do not aspire to positions of great leadership. A lot of women with enormous talent have chosen lesser roles because of the pressures involved in leadership positions or the probability of ever attaining it at all. To reach the top position in the academic world one has to have been a faculty member, probably a department chair, possibly an associate dean, certainly a vice-president, before there is any reasonable expectation of becoming a president. Each of these positions represents a hurdle and very few college or university presidents of either sex set out to become president. They set out to become a professor in a discipline and along the way became interested in administration. Women have to be willing and able in terms of family, professional commitments, and health, to make the increasingly demanding commitments. Most women are not prepared to do this.

Tradition

Certain traditions exist in the academic world of higher education. Chancellors and presidents are taken from the top ranks in academe. Because of social pressure males have been reluctant to advance females. As a result women are often not represented in the top ranks of scholars. The historical model for advancement in higher education has been one in which the young scholar was taken under the tutelage of the older scholar and introduced around the network in a particular field and was then recommended for advancement. The social pressures from male dominated disciplines were for a long time enough to make any scholar reluctant to advance the female. As a result, women didn't move for many years through the traditional ranks.

When legislation began opening the doors for women there weren't many in higher education prepared to step into those leadership roles. The paths women take into higher education frequently don't prepare them to be considered for an administrative post. Females generally don't pursue the kind of disciplines that can build self-assurance for the fiduciary responsibilities of executive work. Historically there has been a lack of awareness among women that leadership roles were potential avenues for them. Therefore they did not prepare themselves or show tremendous interest in getting administrative positions.

Women's Roles

Society has a collective value system that still supports traditional roles for men and women. This value system views women who achieve in nontraditional ways as exceptions to the rule. Many women feel like superwomen because they are expected to. Complaints about the difficulty of handling several roles get the response "you chose it" from both males and females, implying they had the choice of one role or the other, and that they should pay the price if they choose both.

Men are rarely, if ever, required to make a choice between career and home. Even more rarely are questions asked about how society could be changed to accommodate structures and systems that support multiple roles for men and for women.

In general, women do not choose academic careers that can help them into leadership positions; they choose teaching or research instead.

Women still are not heavily into the traditional disciplines of math, science, and engineering that men pursue—disciplines that ultimately lead to executive posts. This observation is supported by the research of Pearson, Shavlik and Touchton who found that of the 1,477 living members of the National Academy of Sciences, only 51 are women.[11] Six were elected in 1975 and 26 since 1975. Early on women have been excluded from exploring science because they were excluded from post-secondary education. This prohibition from training and working in the sciences has continued into the 20th Century, and continues to be a problem on a more subtle level. Women earned almost 40 percent of the bachelor's degrees and about 25 percent of higher degrees in science in 1980, but in 1984, women made up only 12 percent of the scientific and engineering labor force. Science and technology remain a male domain.

Lack of Awareness

A common belief is that women who are really good scholars are likely to be advised into taking a research track and not rewarded for their academic leadership capability. Women are told to go into research and because males have not been socialized to recognize that women are capable of holding greater positions, that's where most women with leadership capability end up.

Boards of trustees or regents are still predominantly male. Men are socialized to think that they can come up through the ranks, assistant to associate to full professor and, if they're lucky, on to assistant dean and dean to vice-president or vice-chancellor, on to president or chancellor. Women do not have the same awareness because they are not taught to think that way.

One chancellor remembered becoming the first woman professor on her campus. Her dean had encouraged her to apply for the title and supported her throughout the process. When she learned the school committee turned in a split vote she was ready to have her name dropped from the list. Her dean, a male, said, "Don't be silly, why pull your name out, the school committee is not the last word, let it go on to the university committee. If you pull out now, you know you're not going to be a full professor. The worst they can tell you is no, they're not going to give it to you. The best they can tell you is sure, here you are." Later her dean told her the title had been awarded to her by a good margin.

Women are no different from men in needing to prepare themselves and recognize opportunities when they occur. They are different from men in that they are not raised to view positions of leadership as possible professional goals.

Women need to perform well on the job more so than men in order to be seen as being ready for the next position, whatever that might be. Only a very small percentage of significant business and professional leadership is in the hands of women today. Awareness of what it takes to be eligible for top leadership must be a priority. Because too few women have made it there is a lack of understanding of what is necessary.

Although some young women say they would like to become a college president, they don't seem to be aware of the need to pay one's dues. There is a sense that if they become the assistant to the president, then the next step will be president. This rarely happens because women often have little or no idea of the rigorous path that must be followed.

Slowing Progress

Women's early ascent to leadership was slowed by poor decision making on the part of those who make appointments. Vestiges of affirmative action for the wrong reasons can still be seen in higher education. When women did begin to choose appropriate educational paths and to aspire to leadership positions, it was felt by those who made such appointments that one woman was as good as any other. This lack of initiative to carefully screen for real leadership capabilities hurt women's opportunities because some women, like some men, are incompetent. This creates a bad image and hurts those who are competent and are attempting to move into roles of greater leadership.

It is also sometimes the case that women become serious about their careers later in life than men. It is not uncommon to see women come back to school to begin or complete their education after raising a family or holding a job to support their spouse's educational aspirations. When this occurs they generally set professional expectations in terms of qualifications and abilities lower because other kinds of demands have been put on their time. It is also true that women who exhibit leadership skills and abilities often become indispensable assets to their bosses who do not want to lose them by providing good recommendations for advancement.

The factors that have kept women from preparing for and getting administrative positions have diminished over the past 10 years. There is a more receptive attitude towards women in leadership positions. But despite the gains women have made in terms of advanced degrees awarded to them, women still constitute a small minority of faculty and administrators in institutions of higher education.

Conclusion

We live in a system which supports a white male power structure. To a large extent this means men are in positions of societal leadership, with the authority to decide what's to be done, and who is to be in charge. This type of environment is not supportive of women who aspire to leadership roles because of the change it would require of the system. It instead reinforces a prejudiced view against those women who do not buy into the status quo. Women who do attempt to gain leadership positions will find barriers placed along their paths to deter them from competition. The social pressures for women to stay within traditional roles and the stereotypes used to support that tradition reinforce a system that supports males in leadership positions.

The other factor that makes it difficult for women to attain leadership positions is that of socialization. Traditionally females are not raised with the expectation of leadership. Therefore, they are often poorly prepared when such an opportunity presents itself. Acceptable roles for women don't address leadership possibilities, and females often aren't aware that they need to choose a different, perhaps more difficult path if they expect some day to aspire to leadership.

10

ABSTRACT

Language, listening skills, non-verbal cues—all play an important part in the communication process. Some studies have shown differences exist between communication behaviors of men and women. Although one style of communication is not necessarily superior to another, history dictates that the male "style" is accepted as more appropriate for leadership positions.

This chapter provides a detailed look at communication in organizations in general and focuses on communication strategies for women in higher education, in particular.

Chapter Ten

Communication Strategies for Women in Higher Education Administration

Karen A. Johnson

*T*he rationale and inspiration for the study of women in higher education administration stems from the existence of a blatant problem with no feasible short-term solutions. Although the numbers of women in administrative positions are increasing, they are still underrepresented. The problem is not simply gender, or being a woman, but attributes that are associated with power and leadership. Pounder notes that "the earnings gap in male and female administrators may be attributed only marginally to gender itself and more directly to job-related factors that tend to vary with gender—that is, position segregation and professional experience profile."[1]

A recent article in the *Chronicle of Higher Education* reports that a hostile climate for women still exists on most college campuses: "Female faculty and staff members are paid less than men who hold jobs of equivalent rank, are more likely to hold lower-level positions, and receive fewer job promotions."[2] Since the climate for women in academe is still poor, the solution is more complex than creating and

KAREN A. JOHNSON is a doctoral candidate in Educational Administration at the University of Southern Mississippi. She holds a B.A. degree from the University of Saskatchewan in Saskatoon, Canada and an M.A. in Speech Communication from the University of Northern Colorado. Ms. Johnson has made several presentations at national conferences on women's issues.

enforcing legislation for equity. "Parity for women in academe is a proper goal. But it will not be achieved by invective or quotas."[3]

The immediate solution lies in individuals and specifically, their control over others' perceptions of them. Effective communication skills are vital to administrators, since they create the perception of a leader. If women become aware of and practice powerful communication skills, they will increase their representation in administrative positions. "It is estimated that between 50 and 93 percent of an executive's day is spent in social interaction."[4] The importance of these interactions cannot be overemphasized; communicative behavior influences perceptions and may contribute to judgments of competence, personality, and expectations of behavior. It is crucial to understand that men and women have different communication styles, but neither is better than the other.[5] However, for roles traditionally occupied by men, the masculine communication style is perceived as more effective. Communication skills are the key to success for women who are seeking jobs, promotions, or more recognition for their vital roles in organizations.

ROLE OF THE ADMINISTRATOR

The literature does not provide a formula for an effective administrator. However, by observing people who have been successful in these positions, certain characteristics and skills can be identified as contributing factors to effective leadership. Speizer reports on an Administrative Skills Program, held annually, which is designed for women in higher education administration. The program focuses on six skill areas for women administrators: fiscal management, organizational behavior, management skills, information management, government and university relations, and professional development (with special emphasis on leadership, human relations, and career mapping).[6] Besides fiscal management, all other areas deal directly or indirectly with communication skills. While a person must possess minimal qualifications to become an administrator, in order to carry out the responsibilities of the position, interacting with, and often persuading, a large number of people on a daily basis is required.

Ongoing skills training in organizations is designed to benefit both males and females, however, one must first be hired; perhaps this is one of the biggest hurdles for women to overcome. "As a general rule, school districts—and all employers—are prohibited from establishing job qualifications that are derived from female stereotyping. The courts have uniformly required employers to prove that any restrictions are indeed bonafide occupational qualifications."[7] Unfortunately, the job qualifications on paper may be quite different from the interviewer's expectations. Legislation appears to be moving towards the inclusion of women, but there are limitations to putting policy into practice. "Policy statements banning discrimination based on sex reduce overt forms of discrimination. Subtle kinds of discriminatory attitudes and behaviors, however, may remain and serve to devalue women's contributions and thwart their potential."[8]

Job qualifications for administrators in higher education, as listed in any issue of the *Chronicle of Higher Education* consistently require: outstanding interpersonal, communication, and organizational skills, providing leadership, team oriented, able to communicate effectively, public speaking and public relations skills, articulate ideas, work effectively with students, faculty, and administrators, proven oral and written communication skills, and human relations skills. A potential employee will most likely be expected to exhibit these skills during the interview process. The key to a successful interview lies in the perceptions of the interviewers—what do they consider to be "effective communication skills?" Can they concretely identify them? Do these skills favor the male or female communication style?

Leadership theories provide some insight into qualities and skills for leaders, but Baughman advises "there is yet to emerge a comprehensive perspective that will describe the ideal manager or leader."[9] Early theories on leadership emphasized traits. Leaders were thought to be born with certain inherent qualities, and others who did not possess these qualities could never learn to be leaders. Height and weight were measured, along with vocabulary, intelligence, and personality tests. Women were automatically excluded because they could never be strong, authoritarian dictators. For example, in 1904 a woman presented a paper to the National Education Association, but the leaders (males) created situations in which woman speakers were ridiculed. They nominated women candidates who were unprepared for public speaking—a requirement in the election process—in order to temporarily undermine their credibility.[10] Almost a century ago, communication was identified as the key to success or failure, and thus became the target for attack.

Eventually, trait theories lost credibility since they did not stand up to systematic study. Research turned to styles of leadership rather than focusing on the leader as a person. Many different styles were identified, but it was found that the purpose of the group and its task determined the ideal style to be used; therefore one person, or style, would not be appropriate all the time. As views of effective leadership changed, women entered the arena, bringing with them new styles of leadership and communication.

Bormann and Bormann studied the emergence concept, or the way a leader emerges during the course of a group working on a task. "It includes the idea that leaders are to some extent born, but it also suggests that potential leaders can acquire skills and improve talents."[11] Based on this information, the authors studied women in small groups. They concluded that female leadership is a culture-bound feature of small group communication, perhaps even unique to the United States. In their simulated studies they also found that men resisted supporting the woman contender who emerged as clearly the best person to be the group leader. Most males resisted female leadership by becoming nonparticipant or apathetic. In other words, even when women do possess excellent leadership and communication skills, stereotypes prevail, and the woman leader must work to overcome them. Bormann and Bormann's overall conclusion is that "the group context and the socialization of its members will often result in women finding resistance, prejudice, and frustrations in their efforts to achieve leadership. However, many of these problems are not inherent sex-linked traits, but matters of socialization that can be changed."[12]

Other studies have looked at masculine and feminine traits in efforts not to overgeneralize about men and women. "Masculinity directly predicts the degree to which women are inclined to express control in interpersonal situations, i.e., to take charge and responsibility...This finding is consistent with previous research that has associated passivity and lack of leadership or assertion with femininity."[13] Masculine qualities, therefore, have historically been associated with leadership.

Some studies "have not found *real* differences in leadership behavior of men and women, differences are *perceived* to exist. Even the attribution of successful performance appears to be influenced differentially by the sex of the actor."[14] If these studies are valid, leadership training will not completely solve the discrimination problem; there appears to be a wider social stereotype of women and leadership which needs to be overcome. In other words, even when there is no difference in communication behaviors between men and women, the perception or expectation of differences essentially creates a difference, at least in the mind of the perceiver. "Apparently males and females appear to see themselves similarly for the most part; however, they are seen as exhibiting fairly distinct male and female communication styles by others or at least are expected to do so."[15]

If a good leader/administrator cannot be measured simply by personal characteristics, an alternative might be to rate him or her on subordinate satisfaction. "We are very touchy about people who boss us around. We do not like to take orders. If we must have a leader, we prefer one who gives wise orders in a way that we can tolerate."[16] In fact, some reports say that morale and job satisfaction are higher when workers are supervised by a woman. One study found that "subjects who had worked with/for a woman manager had more positive attitudes toward women in management than did subjects without work experience with women managers."[17] Apparently, some people will make competency judgments without ever having experienced a woman manager. Unfortunately, these may be the same people who make hiring, promotion, and salary decisions.

COMMUNICATION SKILLS

Perception and Self Concept

Self concept is a set of relatively stable perceptions each of us holds about ourselves.[18] Our self concept develops and changes throughout our lifetime and is influenced by many events, mostly the feedback we receive from people we hold in high regard, or significant others. Our self concept will determine how we communicate with others—passive, assertive, or aggressive people interact in different ways—thus reflecting how we feel about ourselves. Additionally, self concept determines how we perceive others and how they perceive us. All of these perceptions become tangible during the communication process. People with low self concepts tend to talk less, appear passive, and also perceive others more negatively. Passive people are rarely found in leadership positions. "If other group members get the impression that a member of the group does not contribute any ideas for the group task or does not contribute toward organizing the group, then the individual will be eliminated as a potential leader of the group. This impression is created by being quiet, vague, tentative and self-effacing, and always asking others for ideas and procedural direction."[19]

For women, perception plays a key role. We need to be aware of how we are presenting ourselves and if this is appropriate for the situation or the perceiver's expectations. For example, in the employment process the interviewer will be looking for certain characteristics, most notably leadership and communication skills. By demonstrating the desired qualities, a woman will be perceived as competent. Unfortunately, "often a stereotype comes into being when a group of traits is erroneously associated with a special body of people. This has been the case with women who strive to achieve leadership roles in a management world once dominated by men."[20]

Obviously we can't change others' perceptions easily. Women can, however, build their own self concept and confidence in knowing that they can do the job. "People's perceptions of their capabilities affect how they behave, their level of motivation, their thought patterns, and their emotional reactions in taxing situations."[21] The problem is that, for women, a catch-22 exists: If you can't be hired for a position in the first place, how can you prove yourself to be an effective leader? Furthermore, it is difficult to retain a high self concept and feeling of self worth when you are unemployed or underemployed. "Much of people's self-esteem is derived from the importance they feel their work has; a perception that often comes from the title of their role."[22]

Language

The language we use reflects how we perceive ourselves, although we are often unaware of our word choices. Socialization plays a large role in determining the language we use.

Early in childhood, girls learn to use conversation as a basis for friendships. For boys, words are used for power, asserting oneself, or keeping the attention of the group. Boys' conversations are filled with commands, put-downs, and competition. Where girls use words as bridges, boys use them as weapons.[23]

Later in life, a similar pattern seems to exist. Tannen notes, "For women, talk is the glue that holds relationships together; it creates connections between people and a sense of community. For men, activities hold relationships together; talk is used to negotiate their position in a group and preserve independence."[24] As we continue to use certain types of words for certain reasons, we develop a language that represents our unique personality.

Recent research in communication focuses away from male-female differences and looks at powerful and powerless language. Researchers are hesitant to connect either style with gender, but Spitzack and Carter note that "given the social polarization of males and females, identical communication behaviors are unlikely."[25]

One of the functions of language is that it reflects power, or the extent to which we are perceived as powerful. Six categories of powerless language have been identified:

Hedges:	"I'm kinda disappointed..."
	"I think we should..."
	"I guess I'd like to..."
Hesitations:	"Uh, can I have a minute of your time?"
	"Well, we could try this idea..."
	"I wish you would -er- try to be on time."
Intensifiers:	"So, that's how I feel..."
	"I'm not very hungry."
Polite Forms:	"Excuse me, sir..."
Tag Questions:	"It's about time we got started, isn't it?"
	"Don't you think we should give it another try?"
Disclaimers:	"I probably shouldn't say this, but..."
	"I'm not really sure, but..."[26]

On the other hand, powerful language uses very few of these forms and it is generally fluent and direct. Further research in this area concludes that "although several theorists have argued for various sorts of connections between powerful/powerless styles and gender...our results provide little support for an association between the two variables."[27] Adler and Rodman explain that "if women generally use "powerless" language, this fact probably reflects their social role in society at large."[28] Since the gender effect is apparently inconclusive, women should identify their style, and work towards a powerful style, at least in leadership roles. "As opportunities for men and women become more equal, we can expect that the differences between male and female use of language will become smaller."[29]

Spitzack and Carter propose that the main gender difference is not language use, but in perception and role expectation. For example, when women use tag questions, they are perceived as passive, lacking in authority, and polite, but when men use tag questions, they are perceived as open and congenial, thus raising their level of competence.[30] When women's speech is measured against "standard" male speech, it will always be found different, and probably deficient. Some researchers suggest that if women can be taught to communicate like men, they will become equally competent. "Effective leadership courses talk about "leading the troops," "managing the men in the field," "competing with hostile forces," and implicitly encourage other such combative qualities. But most women managers do not want to adopt stereotypical male behavior and strategies to achieve their aims."[31] Tannen notes that "women and men would both do well to learn strategies more typically used by members of the other group—not to switch over entirely, but to have more strategies at their disposal."[32]

Others' language use also affects our self concept, such as the use of racist and sexist language. Although the user will often claim that these words are used in "fun" or jokingly, it does not negate the impact they have on the self concept of those facing discrimination. Even when sexist language is used unintentionally, it still influences perception. After studying the generic masculine, Martyna concluded that "in fact, explorations of our understanding of the generic masculine have demonstrated that 'he' is an ambiguous term which often allows a specifically male interpretation to be drawn from an intended generic usage."[33] The historical use of "he" is no justification for continued use; generic language is much more inclusive and acceptable.

Listening Skills

Contrary to popular belief, listening is a skill, not a trait, and so it can be learned and improved. Most of us take listening for granted, when, in reality, we are very poor listeners. In the author's study on listener characteristics and listening skills, no significant gender difference in listening ability was found.[34]

There is a difference, however, in the gender of the speaker, and how well they are listened to. Gruber and Gaebelein's study found that when a man and woman say the same thing, more attention will be paid to what the man says than to what the woman says. Both male and female listeners remembered more from speeches given by the men. The authors conclude that, "stated simply, the notion of sex-role stereotyping implies that women are not supposed to be as competent as men, particularly in skills and activities that men typically engage in."[35] In this case, the activity was public speaking.

Duerst-Lahti studied conversational dynamics in a decision-making group of administrators, and noted that women are not necessarily "frozen out" of conversation or dismissed as ineffective if they refuse to let men dominate the conversation. "Most of these women appear to have mastered coverbal power displays. They took more than their share of turns of the floor, won verbal challenges, and managed to get their issues into the final product."[36] However, she notes that these women likely did not exhibit behaviors found in a general population of women, or they would not have achieved the positions they held if they did. Perhaps listeners are more attentive to a certain communication style, and do not distinguish between male and female speakers.

Other studies report that people listen for different information; women listen for feelings and men listen for facts. "It may be, given what we know of the values that males and females carry into their jobs in schools, that the woman is focused upon an instructional issue or a matter concerning the [student], whereas the man has chosen to discuss an administrative problem."[37]

Being an active (as opposed to passive) listener is vital for feedback. An effective administrator must be open to feedback, and even actively seek it out. Feedback provides one with rewards, uncertainty reduction, error detection, secondary reinforcement, knowledge of results, information about a unit's performance, and motivation for correction.[38] It is interesting to note that people with low self-esteem perform worse after negative feedback, but if they are given positive feedback, performance improves.

Nonverbal Communication

"While men appear to excel in the verbal area of communication, at least in terms of dominance, women tend to excel in the nonverbal area."[39] For example, women are more likely to be good decoders of nonverbal expressions, they can more accurately judge emotions from voice cues. Since women more often listen for feelings, they are also likely to respond to them.

As listeners, women tend to give more signals such as saying yes, um-hmmm, and exhibiting interested facial expressions. Men's faces are usually passive, even when they are actively listening. While listening, men will try to find a solution (analyzing), while women listen more for emotions. When men say yes or um-hmmm, this means they agree, whereas women do this simply to show they are listening.[40]

During conversation, men definitely interrupt more, and Robinson and Reis found that interrupters were seen as less sociable, but also more assertive, more traditionally masculine, and less feminine than those who did not interrupt. On the other hand, those who were interrupted (usually women) "were seen as less assertive, more traditional, more emotionally vulnerable, and less masculine than controls."[41]

Other differences in male and female nonverbal communication include touch; men touch women considerably more frequently than women touch men. This often gets interpreted as dominance, because higher-status, dominant individuals tend to touch lower-status, subordinates more than the reverse. Women need to be aware that "her touch is likely to be interpreted as having a sexual meaning regardless of her intention."[42] In terms of distance, men prefer a greater distance between themselves and another person, while there tends to be a smaller distance between women and others. These "rules" are ambiguous, but they convey strong messages.

In regard to facial expression, women smile more than men. These findings have been difficult to interpret, but it seems that women smile when they are happy, nervous, uncomfortable, or just empathizing with another person. Men smile when they are happy. Another important facial cue is eye contact. Women spend more time gazing at their conversation partner than men do. "Interpretations have generally revolved around (1) women's traditional orientation toward the social world and interpersonal relations or (2) the use of eye contact in order to gain approval and/or cues regarding the appropriateness of behavior."[43]

Nonverbal signals are very influential in shaping perceptions, and often this is unconscious. Therefore, "an exceptionally talented women may not be hired for an administrative position because she is 'nice and petite' and does not measure up to the image of a strong leader held by those in a position to hire her."[44] Although women have little control over their physical attributes, females in managerial positions have often been encouraged to dress professionally. They end up being dressed like men; in dark colors, high necklines, low-heeled shoes, and the female version of a business suit. Dressing in this manner leads women to be perceived as more competent, credible, and capable. This trend is discouraging in light of Tannen's statement that "furthermore, if women's and men's styles are shown to be different, it is usually women who are told to change."[45] What happened to the "equally valid styles?" Tannen also says that "pretending that women and men are the same hurts women, because the ways they are treated are based on the norms for men."[46]

The implications of communication for females in administration seems promising. As far as interpersonal communication is concerned, women tend to be more skilled and thus should be perceived as better people managers than males. If the trend towards more humanistic management continues, along with the integration of women into top positions, we should see an eventual decrease in gender discrimination. "Thus the movement away from the formalistic and towards the participative management model should mean that women move into decision-taking and decision-making posts."[47] In higher education, "campuses may be more willing to examine their environments as more of their senior female administrators and professors push for women's issues."[48]

COMMUNICATION IN ORGANIZATIONS

Administrative and Bureaucratic Models

Often when we look at the formal structure of organizations, which are so important and so totally controlling, we wonder how much impact or influence one individual's communication skills can have. Organizations attach clear verbal and nonverbal labels to the status of positions. Outsiders can easily tell the status of any given person by looking at verbal titles such as dean, director, manager, supervisor, professor, etc., as well as nonverbal cues such as location and size of their offices, number of secretaries, furniture, etc. Status is also portrayed in an organizational chart. These charts plot the hierarchy and thus the degree of power and control that an individual possesses.

There currently exists a strict hierarchy in institutions of higher education. Although each varies slightly, the blueprint is essentially the same. The president (9.4 percent are women) is at the top of the hierarchy, with provosts (13.6 percent women) and academic deans (13.8 percent women) reporting to him. As we get lower in the hierarchy, women are more visible in positions like librarians (34.2 percent) and financial aid (35.5 percent).[49] "An underlying requirement for each of these functions is an efficient concept of vertical communication following the chain of command so that the manager would have the necessary information with which to make decisions."[50]

It will be important for any administrator to be aware of, and use both the formal and informal communication channels that exist horizontally and vertically within the hierarchical structure. Lately, there has been more emphasis on horizontal communication flow, which relies on the informal relationships between members. Interpersonal communication is the vehicle for information transfer between people.

Formal communication channels operate in conjunction with the hierarchy; it is designed to be planned and logical. While originally strictly vertical, formal channels have become lateral also. Formal group meetings and oral messages are as important as written policies or memos.

Informal channels of communication are often seen as a response to the formalized rules and procedures. Sometimes called the "grapevine," information tends to travel much more quickly, but not necessarily more accurately than through the formalized channels. Informal communication is sometimes called gossip. Gossip usually carries a negative connotation, but it isn't always necessarily destructive. The distinction between gossip and rumor needs to be clear—rumors have no basis in fact and are often destructive. Gossip can be likened more to small talk. Tannen gives an example of productive gossip in the workplace:

> A woman who runs a counseling center noted that when she meets with women on her staff, it is not unusual for them to spend 75 percent of the time in personal talk and then efficiently take care of business in the remaining 25 percent. To men on the staff, this seems like wasting time. But the director places value on creating a warm, intimate working environment. She feels that such personal talk contributes to a sense of rapport that makes the women on her staff happy in their jobs and lays a foundation for the working relationship that enables them to conduct business so efficiently.[51]

Therefore, although bureaucratic policy and organizational charts attempt to instill formal lines of communication in an institution, the informal lines must be taken seriously, as they are a powerful interpersonal connection between all of the individuals working there.

> Such considerations as the structured network of information flow, the filtering of messages, the direction of information between superiors, subordinates, and peers, the effects of organizational culture in both the internal and external environment, and the influence of formal and informal emergent behaviors all form a fabric which is communication within the organization.[52]

Conflict and Decision Making

Traditionally, organizational conflict was seen as something to be avoided at all costs, as it would disrupt the working harmony in an organization. Many people also feel this way about conflict in interpersonal relationships. However, more recent research shows that conflict in either situation is both valuable and necessary. Conflict creates challenges, innovation, and change, which can all work to the benefit of an organization. Finally, conflict is inevitable, so administrators need to learn to turn these situations into productive ones; the critical element is using an effective communication style to accomplish this. There are many ways of dealing with conflict, but the least effective is the use of higher authority imposing a solution in favor of one conflicting group.[53]

As in conversation, men and women typically deal with conflict in different ways. Tannen feels that "to most women, conflict is a threat to connection, to be avoided at all costs. Disputes are preferably settled without direct confrontation. But to many men, conflict is the necessary means by which status is negotiated, so it is to be accepted and may even be sought, embraced, and enjoyed."[54] This observation is in reference to participating in conflict, and it is unfair to generalize this tendency to women in leadership positions working as conflict mediators. They may behave quite differently when acting as the third party.

The way in which anyone deals with conflict can be linked to his or her leadership style. Lyons talks about Mary Parker Follett's 1930 writings on organizations. She saw that conflict could be addressed in three ways: by domination, by compromise, or by creative integration. She favored the latter, emphasizing the importance of the psychology of the relationships between people in conflict. Apparently, Follett's ideas were ahead of their time, as they were not embraced quickly.[55] Her ideas closely resemble the recent interest in collaborative models of decision-making. When adopting this style of management, a leader needs to keep in mind the need for long-term collaboration, or participants may see this style as manipulation rather than collaboration.[56]

Since collaborative decision making and conflict both involve interpersonal interaction between those involved, and possibly a mediator, effective communication skills will be vital to a manager in order to reach agreement. When women do confront conflict, they seem to deal with it in a less authoritative style than do men. "Women's inclination to seek agreement may even be an advantage in management. Many people feel that women make better managers because they are more inclined to consult others and involve employees in decision making, and everyone agrees that employees are more likely to implement a policy efficiently if they feel they have played a part in making it."[57]

On the other hand, it seems that a workplace with an abundance of conflict may be a difficult place for conflict-avoiders to work. Long's 1989 study on women in non-traditional occupations (such as administration) found high feminine women to have lower levels of self-efficacy, greater strain, and more coping difficulties than low-feminine women. Her study implies that organizations need to attend to these personality factors. "Such a view supports personal-based interventions oriented toward enhancing self-efficacy and sex-role expectations, while developing adaptive coping strategies. At the same time, it fosters environmental interventions designed towards ameliorating stressful organizational structures."[58] Stressful organizational structures may well be a result of the hierarchy developed by men, for men.

Hanna's 1988 article looks at organizational decision making specifically in the area of affirmative action. The impact of the 1972 Higher Education Guidelines for areas affected by affirmative action is discussed. She found that leadership from the top administrator was the most often named positive influence in terms of supporting affirmative action at all institutions studied. Unfortunately, "their commitment is insufficient by itself, however, because faculty affirmative action requires fundamental changes in hiring, retention, and promotion decisions—decisions that are made by faculty in departments. The ability of administrative leaders to set an institutional agenda is one of their most powerful tools...and this is the essence of decentralization in the university: faculty making critical judgments about other faculty."[59] Thus, administrators have limited power, except to establish policy and develop supporting procedures. Hanna notes that this may be why affirmative action has appeared to be a slow process, because decentralized change itself is slow.

CONCLUSION

A common thread throughout the literature is that discrimination is embedded in socialization, and in the expectations for males and females. The solution must lie in changing society's attitudes, and destroying stereotypes. Several studies have suggested that as women become fully integrated into the work force, these stereotypes will diminish. However, history has shown us that the process is slow, and can even take backward turns. If higher education is really proactive with respect to social change, institutions should be at the forefront of equality, presenting the ideal to business, industry, and the wider society. "Nowhere is the disparity between ideal and practice more damaging to the meritocratic charter of educational institutions than in the underrepresentation of women and minorities in administrative positions. These positions are highly visible; they signal institutional commitment to equity for all other units within the organization."[60]

The immediate solution lies in the individual, specifically women, to prove themselves equal to or more competent than men in leadership positions. The question arises: What constitutes adequate representation for women? The answer is unclear; it is difficult to establish a number or percentage of women administrators as a goal. Research shows that men are one and one-half times more likely to complete doctoral degrees than women. Women should not be hired simply to fill an EEO quota, but should be judged on their qualifications as objectively as possible. Sylvia notes that "the issue is one of progress and empowerment through education, rather than through position attainment alone."[61] She suggests that the only long-term solution is to increase the number of female applicants for administrative positions, and this is done by recruiting and educating more females.

Progress for women has resulted in overt discrimination being suppressed to subtle forms. For example, Roger Rosenblatt gives a man's perspective on sexual bigotry in the workplace: "In the 1990s, men are finally beginning to realize that the women's movement has moved; it has happened...Some men take the news well, some grudgingly, some angrily. Some take it angrily who only appear to take it well."[62] Rosenblatt believes that men who belittle women do so out of fear that women will prove more capable than them.

Examining the role of an administrator provides some insight into the expectations for hiring and promotion. Achieving the necessary knowledge, skills, and education to perform an administrator's duties will allow women to compete for higher level jobs.

Effective communication skills are invaluable to anyone in a leadership position. Although one style of communication is not necessarily better than another, history dictates that the male "style" is seen as more appropriate for leadership positions. Women need to be aware of, and even able to employ either style when the situation demands. "Whether or not organizations will come to recognize the overall effectiveness of female approaches remains to be seen. For now, women must partially conform to gender expectations, and put forth more effort than men, if they are to achieve high levels of policy influence."[63]

ABSTRACT

If we are successfully to restructure higher education to be more responsive to our dynamic, global society, women must join the higher education leadership ranks at a faster rate. The formidable barriers to diversity created by traditional bureaucratic structures in higher education must be overcome for women to have an opportunity to serve as role models for the increasingly diverse student populations and to add their voices as equal partners in leadership as opposed to partners-on-the-periphery for the future of higher education. To overcome these barriers, women leaders must understand and know how to acquire and use the politics of power while protecting and preserving ethical, nurturing and humanistic leadership qualities.

This chapter is about power, politics, and the continuing challenge to women. It will focus on a strategic plan to direct one's path to power, review procedures for assessing political and cultural climates (power structures) in the work environment using an array of models as frames of reference, and provide insight into ways of gaining entry into, and effectively operating within, the power structure.

Chapter Eleven

Power and Politics:
The Leadership Challenge

Anita J. Harrow

Let us not seek to satisfy our thirst for freedom by drinking from the cup of bitterness and hatred. We must forever conduct our struggle on the high plain of dignity and discipline...

Dr. Martin Luther King, Jr.

We hope to avail the nation of those talents which nature has sown as liberally among the poor as the rich, but which perish without use, if not sought for and cultivated.

Thomas Jefferson

ANITA J. HARROW joined the graduate teaching faculty as Associate Professor and Director of the College Teaching and Leadership Development Program in the Educational Leadership Department at Florida State University after serving in leadership positions at community colleges for over twenty years. She previously served as Vice President for Instruction and Provost of the West Campus at Valencia Community College in Orlando, Florida; Dean of Academic Services at St. Petersburg Junior College in St. Petersburg, Florida; Director of Academic Affairs and Resource Development Officer at Seminole Community College in Sanford, Florida; and as a classroom instructor in secondary, postsecondary, and graduate education programs. She received her A.A. degree from St. Petersburg Junior College, B.A. degree at the University of South Florida, and M.S. and Ph.D. at Florida State University.

INTRODUCTION

A vast array of challenges face higher education in the 21st Century—
one being to incorporate diversity within the leadership structures and
professional staffs at our nation's colleges and universities. Retrench-
ment, competition, promotion/tenure policies, institutional politics
are all hurdles to professional survival, growth, and advancement in
our higher education institutions as well as barriers which continue
to be of prime concern for women seeking leadership roles. Recent
economic conditions and declining public confidence in higher education have exacerbated opportunities for women to move forward into
these leadership positions. Though Naisbitt and Aburdene call the
1990s a decade of career mobility for women, advancement and support
for leadership positions in higher education will continue to be a
challenge for women seeking to rise above the "glass ceiling."[1]

If we are to successfully restructure higher education to be more
responsive to our dynamic, global society, women must join the higher
education leadership ranks at a faster rate. The formidable barriers to
diversity created by traditional bureaucratic structures in higher
education must be overcome for women to have an opportunity to
serve as role models for the increasingly diverse student populations
and to add their voices as equal partners in leadership as opposed to
partners-on-the-periphery for the future of higher education. To overcome these barriers, women leaders must understand and know how
to acquire and use the politics of power while protecting and preserving
ethical, nurturing and humanistic leadership qualities.

This chapter is about power, politics, and the continuing challenge
to women. It will focus on a strategic plan to direct one's path to power,
review procedures for assessing political and cultural climates (power
structures) in the work environment using an array of models as frames
of reference, and will provide insight into ways of gaining entry into,
and effectively operating within, the power structure.

Before beginning our discussion of power and politics, let us explore
some assumptions and definitions upon which this chapter is based.
They are as follows:

1. All institutions, work environments, professional organizations are strong "political arenas that house a complex variety
   of individuals and interest groups."[2]
2. "The world of most managers and administrators is a world
   of complexity, ambiguity, value dilemmas, political pressures,
   and multiple constituencies."[3]
3. No one will ensure equal opportunities for women to acquire
   and retain leadership positions in higher education; gaining
   equal opportunities requires strategic planning and full support.

4. Power use and abuse for personal gain and self interest is a reality which occurs often in higher education.

5. Due process and just cause, legal terms, provide no protection against unscrupulous use of power.

6. Doing an outstanding job is not enough to ensure advancement or job security.

It is important to define some terms. First, what is power? Gardner defines power as the capacity to bring about certain intended consequences in the behaviors of others; it is the capacity to ensure desired outcomes are accomplished and to prevent unwanted outcomes from occurring. Thus, the person in power has authority to exercise control, to act, to force an issue or special interest.[4] "Power is ethically neutral;" it is how power is used that makes the difference.[5]

What constitutes a political process? Gardner defines the political process as "taking into account the needs of diverse constituencies, weighing the realities of power, calculating consequences, negotiating, and bargaining."[6] According to Bolman and Deal, an organization applying a political leadership approach uses the pursuit of self-interest and power as the basic process. The political organization needs power and needs "to be prepared for conflict as a part of the process." Power and political process are inextricably linked throughout the literature on leadership. Women must thoroughly understand and accept this important relationship as they prepare for and attain leadership roles.[7]

Alvin Toffler, in his book, *Power Shift*, reveals an emerging new system for building wealth in the 21st Century which is "based no longer on muscle but on mind."[8] Powershift, in this sense, "is deep-level change in the very nature of power."[9] The basic tools of power are knowledge, wealth, violence and their interrelationships. Toffler makes a clear distinction between quantity and quality of power. Women interested in career mobility must have the knowledge and skills to successfully operate within the power structure while maintaining their integrity as they journey toward their career goals. Thus, the challenge for women in higher education is to learn to assess correctly the nature of power conflicts and analyze the different contenders in the power struggles surrounding them to determine "who commands access to which of the basic tools of power."[10]

Leadership positions not only require the individual to skillfully and ethically use power but, also, to understand the many political arenas surrounding issues. Logically then, the next question is, how does one become politically astute and learn to successfully "play the game"?

Even with the current power shifts in government, business, and society, the transformation of leadership diversity in higher education will not occur without considerable effort. Institutions of higher education are composed of an array of diverse political entities which must be recognized and handled with political acumen. To become equal partners in leadership for the future of higher education, women must possess a critical awareness of the political work environment and must begin building a quality powerbase for career mobility. The skills required for this leadership transformation include astutely assessing political and cultural climates in the work environment; conscientiously building substantive internal and external support systems for career protection and advancement; and earnestly developing communication skills for effectively using power language and listening for hidden agendas.

Finally, we need to ask, "Must women, aspiring to enter the leadership ranks, align their leadership styles to become more like male colleagues? Gender differences in leadership style, if they truly exist, are not crucial. Effective leadership style should fit the culture of the organization or institution. Therefore, it is essential to assess the work environment or culture to determine the leadership style which will produce the best results rather than to blindly imitate the style of others. Leadership style is a dynamic, complex composition of personality characteristics and a combination of acquired skills. Throughout history, women and men have successfully served in leadership positions demonstrating a diversity of styles. Leaders whose performances made a difference were considered effective, regardless of gender. Though men currently represent the majority in higher education leadership positions, it is not because they are more effective as leaders than women. It is because men have more opportunities for entrance into top-level leadership roles and have established quality power-bases for career mobility.

Some years ago when addressing the Association of Women in Science, Estelle Ramey, then President of the association, said,

> I have worked all my life with men, and I have discovered that some of them are very smart, some of them are very stupid, and most of them are mediocre hacks. Women fall into the same categories. We will have equality when a female schlemiel moves ahead as fast as a male schlemiel. That's equality, not when Marie Curie gets promoted to Associate Professor.[11]

These words are worth remembering now as women seek advancement and later when they help other competent future leaders advance.

WHY SHOULD WE CHANGE?

There are those who question the need to change from the dominant leadership structures now operational in higher education to a more diverse structure for the new century. Why is it so important for women to have a voice in leadership? In this dynamic, ever-changing society, the nation in the 21st Century will be compelled to have leaders in higher education prepared to deal with large scale diversity, advancing technology, and an array of changes in social and economic problems. It is time for new voices, new perspectives, new strategies, new ways of working with people; all qualified individuals capable of making significant contributions to the advancement of higher education must have an opportunity to serve. Women are part of this valuable national resource and therefore, must represent a significant part of higher education leadership positions. The American Council on Education's Commission on Women reports that:

> The status of women in our society has changed pro-
> foundly over the last two decades. The fundamental
> nature of the changes is inescapable. Women are the
> majority of all students in higher education. The
> numbers of women in the paid work force have vastly
> increased. Women are present to some degree in vir-
> tually every occupational field. They are an influential
> force in the electorate. They are recognized and courted
> as powerful consumers. They have introduced new
> vocabulary and concepts to everyday life. And, they
> have caused society to question traditional notions
> about sex roles and cultural expectations.[12]

Even with the changes in the status of women these past few decades, there remains insufficient leadership diversity in higher education. A 1990 study, conducted by the Office of Federal Contract Compliance Programs of 31,187 managers of 94 Fortune 1000 companies found 16.9 percent were women and 6 percent minorities. Among 4,491 top-level executives, 6.6 percent were women and 2.5 percent minorities.[13] The statistics for women in top-level administrative positions in the nation's colleges and universities are as bleak! When investigating the status of women faculty in higher education, Hensel found that more than 50 percent of the undergraduates are women, 25 percent of the higher education faculty are women, 10 percent of all tenured professors are women, and it takes two to ten years longer for women to be promoted than men.[14] Where are the role models for young college and university women today who are tomorrow's leaders? Why does this rich, progressive nation allow a valuable resource— women capable of working as team members for a better tomorrow— to be barred from higher education leadership ranks?

One need only read the *Chronicle of Higher Education* and other newspapers, national and local, and to listen to national and local news broadcasts to recognize the problems of higher education and the lack of moral and ethical standards in the leadership ranks of government, business, industry and, yes, even at many institutions of higher learning. Leadership, when dominated by one segment of society, suffers from a narrow perspective, a lack of richness of ideas and ideals. Unrepresentative, unresponsive, self-serving, scandalous leadership interferes with institutional vitality and advancement, and serves as a major barrier to leadership diversity. True leaders are those who move beyond themselves to a cause that is just and right, from self-interest, self-serving to focusing upon the stated mission and institutional goals. True leaders empower and promote others into positions of authority in an effort to maximize the benefits accruing from leadership diversity. There is little reason to be in a leadership position unless you can make a difference.

Leaders must not be viewed by gender or race, but valued for the personal assets and strengths they bring to the position. Though men still have control of leadership positions, the question is for how long? Helgesen points out that major societal changes in global competition, advancing technology, and increasing numbers of women in the work force will lead to an increasing demand for leadership styles which promote productivity through empowerment and community within the work environment. She suggests that the warrior age of leadership is at an end—being replaced by leaders with more nurturing, humanistic qualities.[15] It is time society stops using the white male standard as a measure of effective leadership; others who do not belong to this group are as capable of leading, given the opportunity. Public demand for diversity and accountability in higher education leadership must be satisfied if America is to maintain its position in this dynamic, changing global economy.

To really make a significant impact for the 21st Century, the changes resulting from the renewed interest in restructuring higher education should not only include a change in curriculum, instructional delivery, and leadership styles, but also, an increase in the number of women serving in top-level administrative positions. Like many things in education, diversifying higher education leadership will occur slowly; therefore, it is essential for women to continue to actively pursue leadership roles, and to maintain persistent pressure on those individuals who have the power to facilitate the change in leadership. Though open job searches exist, they are few and hard to find. Gaining entry into top level leadership positions has been difficult for women in the past and will get no easier in the future. Women must have the credentials and essential competencies, the right connections, a political savvy in terms of job search and the interview process, and be vigilant in their quest for obtaining rewarding leadership positions.

WHAT IS THE PROCESS?

Gender-oriented political systems have evolved over the centuries with women largely being excluded from the male system. Loden describes the feminine style of management being based in communication, cooperation, and consensus building; while competitiveness, hierarchical structure, and aiming to win are the foundation of masculine management style.[16] Melia describes the feminine socio-political system as based on an easily controllable limited environment, exclusion of anyone or thing perceived as threatening, and dependent on males for security and protection. In contrast, she describes the masculine-oriented political system as based on cooperation, competition, bargaining, and mutual goals. Both authors agree the male system is dependent on effective team play, comraderie, and trust.[17] According to Melia, too few women have developed these traits and thus are excluded from challenging leadership positions.[18]

Even if women developed leadership styles similar to their male colleagues, they are not guaranteed entrance into leadership positions; these gender-based traits, whether important to leadership abilities or not, exist and have powerful implications for limiting women's advancement. As women leaders functioning in complex male-dominated organizations, they still have to deal with competing interests, multiple agendas, and traditional operating values and styles. There are still lessons women must learn about getting to the top and staying there.

> The ability to take risks, accept the consequences, learn from failure, design a new strategy and try again is a difficult trait for many women to master. As a result...women often maintain an inflexible posture and follow rules as law, instead of helping to draft new rules, being a team player, applying patience and regrouping quickly when the chips fall elsewhere—skills men tend to grasp more easily. That may be because men typically are raised to take risks, to put team goals above individual goals and to keep an emotional detachment from organizational effort.[19]

Until there is support and societal sanctions for women to enter top level leadership positions in higher education, women will have to continue the struggle to make strides in the present leadership arena. To be successful, women must learn how to function effectively within the work environment attempting to overcome the many barriers to top positions. This will require analysis of the situation, recognition of the important players, and a strategic plan to achieve individual career goals while satisfying team goals. As more women serve in powerful, decision-making positions, perhaps the needed metamorphosis of leadership will occur. Until that time, wise women will design a comprehensive strategic plan to guide them toward their goals.

THE PLAN

Acquiring a leadership position requires a record of achievement, a plan for career advancement, and a strong, powerful support web. Establishment of a plan to gain a strong power base and support web is critical and should begin early in one's career. A well-devised and implemented plan for advancement into leadership positions does not guarantee a top level position, but will make a more viable competitor, help to overcome the many currently existing barriers, and enhance opportunities for career mobility. The questions are: What are the essential components of this strategic plan for advancement and how does one go about implementing the plan to advance into leadership positions?

There are many different ways to prepare for competition with those seeking top level leadership positions in higher education. The author offers this plan (see Figure 1 below) which is fairly simple in

Figure 1

Strategic Plan for Career Advancement

Phase I: Foundation
      Competence: Establish a knowledge base. Analyze your skills and abilities.

      Political Climate: Analyze the climate in the work environment. Cultivate boss-subordinate relationship.

Phase II: Support Systems
      Web: Identify internal and external coalitions and alliances important to your success.

      Support Team: Select several powerful mentors. Select a confidant.

Phase III: Reaching Career Goal
      Marketing Scheme: Plan your public persona and ways to ensure your voice is heard.

design, but requires dedication to a cause, commitment of time and effort, and a "burning passion" to win.

Scot Hamilton, the Olympic figure skating champion, when asked what is the winning formula for champions said, "It is 50 percent training, 35 percent luck, and 15 percent selfishness."[20] Though these figures may not be relevant for women seeking leadership positions, it is important to note the last component of the formula—selfishness; women too often fail to recognize that not only must they be concerned about the empowerment and nurturing of others, but also promotion and advancement of themselves.

PHASE 1: BUILDING THE FOUNDATION

Establishing a Knowledge Base

Establishing a strong knowledge base is essential for leadership. This requires knowing what information is important and how to maintain a constant flow of usable information coming to you in a timely fashion. Just having information is not enough; it becomes valuable only when it is used to achieve a desired outcome. Korda and Toffler agree that selecting and using the right information puts a leader on the path to increased power and ultimately increased ability to negotiate and bargain.[21] Therefore, it is important to identify the flow of communications and to position yourself for access to essential information and support to ensure success and survival.

> **Rule of Thumb**
> Do your homework.
> Think analytically.
> Take action—do something.

Analyzing the Political Climate

Seeking advancement into leadership roles requires skill and ability in analyzing yourself, the environment, and the other players.

First, understand yourself. Pearson's *Awakening the Heros Within*, though a guide for self-understanding and personal growth, is a useful tool for understanding the different heroic archetypes present within a work environment and for assessing your progress through the archetypes as you focus on your career goals.[22] Understanding the different heroic paths helps you better assess your own actions and understand the motivations and actions of those with whom you work. This valuable information provides you with a level of flexibility and freedom to choose approaches when structuring interactive situations to enhance your chances of working more effectively with colleagues and of accomplishing your goals.

Pearson's 12 heroic archetypes each with its own unique qualities pass through three stages of the hero's journey—Preparation, Journey, and Return. In the Preparation stage which encompasses the first four archetypes, the reader learns to survive in the world as it exists—developing self confidence and becoming productive individuals with high ethical and moral standards. In the Journey stage which encompasses the next group of four archetypes, we are strengthened by the discovery of self worth and value. In the final stage, the Return, we learn to express our true self and transform our lives. Pearson's developmental process could be viewed as analogous to our proposed plan for career advancement; first, you prepare for the journey toward your career goal by establishing a solid foundation and an understanding of the realities of politics in work environments; next, you start the journey by becoming actively involved in the political realities of the work environment strengthening your skills and abilities and your position by building interconnected support systems; and finally, you reach your career goal.

Figure 2

Comparison of Pearson's Stages with Career Plan

Pearson's Stages of Hero's Journey[23]	*Strategic Career Planning*
Preparation	Foundation
Innocent-Orphan	Knowledge Bases
Warrior-Caregiver	Political Climates
Journey	Support Systems
Seeker-Lover	Webs
Destroyer-Creator	Support Teams
	Marketing Scheme
Return	Career Goal
Ruler-Magician	Transformer
Sage-Fool	

After you have a thorough understanding of your strengths and have done something about skills and abilities needing improvement, you move to the second step which is analyzing the climate in which you are working. To successfully climb the career ladder, you must work effectively with people. Until you become president of the institution, remember the political reality that the boss sets the pace and establishes the emotional climate in the work environment; he or she has an established leadership style which will not be changed for the convenience of subordinates. Since the boss usually has total control of your destiny on the job and ultimately, your career advancement at the institution, it is essential that you work smart and establish an effective boss/subordinate relationship.

Early in your career cultivate the skill of effectively working with people; it is an essential tool for advancement. Gabarro and Kotter provide a framework for analyzing administrative leadership styles and for establishing an effectively functioning boss/subordinate relationship. They claim the boss/subordinate relationship evolves from mutual dependence essential for success.[24]

Next, recognize who possesses power, how it is distributed, and how it is used in the work environment. Careful analysis of the political climate enhances success and facilitates advancement. Armed with the knowledge about the power structure and the key players, you are better prepared to negotiate or cope with everyday political realities and plan strategically for future advancement. Ready access to and comfortable relationships with powerful people are essential to career advancement. Build power bases and political support webs early before

Figure 3

Organizational Frames

Frame	Some Characteristics
Structural Frame	Management hierarchies Division of labor Run by goals, rules, policies, etc.
Human Resource Frame	Concern for individual needs/concerns Comfortable work environment Tailor organization to people
Political Frame	Power and influence affect resource allocation Bargaining, coercion, compromise central to work environment Political skill and acumen are essential
Symbolic Frame	Lacks rationality apparent in other frames Run by rituals, ceremonies, etc. Held together by shared values and culture

Source: Adapted from Modern Approaches to Understanding and Managing Organizations, *Borman and Deal (1984) pp. 4-7.*

they are needed. Women should begin building power bases early in their careers and include it among the first activities when accepting a leadership position.

As noted in Figure 3, Bolman and Deal's—structural, human resource, political, and symbolic approaches to understanding and managing organizations, provide valuable insight and are easily applied to assess leadership style, power use, and work culture climate. The authors caution, however, that all organizations are multiple realities and can be viewed through several frames of reference.[25]

Since all organizations contain multiple realities, it is not uncommon to find different leadership styles and work environments at different levels and within different departments of an organization. Concentrate on the people and departments important to your functioning and success and be sure you have a clear understanding of the political dynamics.

Finally, make yourself a valued, trusted member of the leadership team. Women usually must work harder for inclusion and retention in the power circle. Be alert; competitors often will resort to any means to take credit for your work and to cause damage to your credibility and position on the team. These power players wear many masks and are sometimes difficult to identify. Always be alert to the political aspect of each situation.

Power comes from many sources and is exercised in a variety of ways. Power stems from position, possessions, charismatic personalities, and physical strength. Though it is important to recognize the source of power, it is more important for success, promotion, and survival to understand how it is being used by those with power in the work environment. Always be alert to improper uses of power. There are many cases of improper use, and in some instances, actual abuse of power. Not only must you learn how to assess power use, but also, how to recognize and cope with abusive power situations. Learn to read the signs before it is too late. Following are some case studies:

Case 1

> Marion, a bright young educator, had served for a number of years in a non-tenure track position as assistant director of a well-funded nationally recognized project. She was a major contributor to the strategic planning for the project and, through her dedication and diligence, successfully implemented the plan designing and using comprehensive systems for record keeping, accountability, and public relations. Though she was a task master, those whom she supervised found her

to be sensitive to their needs, consistent, and fair, sharing in the workload as well as the accolades for a job well done. Through her support and efforts, the project received high acclaim and national visibility. She proved to be a loyal, dedicated member of the project team working to achieve the stated project goals.

The project director, an equally outstanding educator, left the project to accept an academic leadership position at a well-known higher eduction institution. A new project director was hired; after being in the position less than a month, Marion was fired and was replaced by one of the director's close friends.

Could this be called an example of an abuse of power? Is it fair or right to deprive a productive, loyal employee of employment just to hire a friend? Because Marion did not have tenure, does that mean she should also be deprived of "due process"?

Though there was probably nothing Marion could have done after the action was taken, with a strong power base she would have been in a more favorable position to negotiate a win-win position for herself.

Case II

Richard, a well-known community college educator whose traditional career path lead him to a high-level administrative position at a large, multi-campus institution, had successfully served as a chief academic officer for several years. When the new president arrived, Richard introduced him to the community power structure, helped him to familiarize himself with the college programs and personnel, and was a highly competent, loyal, dedicated colleague.

The president's strength was fund-raising and community support while Richard's strength lay in academic programs and personnel. The two were a great team and things moved smoothly for a number of years. Occasionally, Richard and the president would disagree on academic matters. One day without explanation or warning, the president told Richard his services were no longer needed at the college, and Richard was immediately removed to serve out his contract away from the college. Richard forgot the old adage, "...he may not be right, but he is the king!"

Perhaps Richard was too quick to place complete trust in his new president. He lost sight of the importance of the boss/subordinate relationship. When he got in trouble, he also lost his power base because he so successfully transferred it to the new president.

Cases such as these raise valid questions. Is this the traditional "good ole boy" network at work? Is there a better way to handle disagreements? Is this situation an example of ethical use of power? How do you protect yourself from this type of leadership behavior and action? Difficult questions, but ones which must be addressed by those currently in a position to make a difference if women are to have equal opportunities for leadership positions.

> **Rule of Thumb**
> Be careful whom you trust.
> Wear the appropriate mask for each occasion.
> Master gamesmenship skills.

PHASE II: SUPPORT SYSTEMS

Weaving a Strong Web

Establishing external as well as internal coalitions and alliances is an extremely important form of job security. Smart leaders relentlessly investigate the community organizations and informal groups with whom strong coalitions could be formed and join those which have the power people important to the institutional mission and to the leaders' success and survival. Once in, smart leaders ensure that their voices are heard as active, supportive members of any organization or group they join.

These external and internal coalitions and alliances become the foundation of a leader's power base. It is, therefore, extremely important for women leaders to begin focusing on the development of both internal and external power bases; a power base differs dramatically from the concepts of mentoring and networking. Mentors serve as advisors, links to advancement, and confidants while networks serve as sources for exchange of information but provide very little strategic planning for career advancement. Power bases are safety nets for survival.

Building power bases takes a good deal of skill and time. Women must learn how to analyze who is in the power sphere, how much impact these players can have on success, and when these players should enter the game to assist or support. Not only do women have to learn how to build power bases, they must understand the strategies for maintaining these power bases to assist them in becoming effective power players while maintaining their own value systems.

Rule of Thumb
Recognize political complexities
in each situation. Build relationships
for advancement and survival.

Choosing the Right Support Team

Selecting mentors is essential for success and upward mobility. Mentors serve a variety of purposes, therefore, seeking several different mentors to assist with specific aspects of professional development and advancement for leaders is a wise career move. Though this is an extremely important part of the strategic plan for career advancement, it is briefly mentioned here since it is covered in greater detail in Chapter 7. Remember, there is a difference between mentors and networks; each serves a different function.

Rule of Thumb
Be smart enough to surround yourself
with dedicated, caring associates.
Actions speak louder than words and are worth more.

PHASE III: REACHING YOUR CAREER GOALS

Marketing Scheme

Once a powerful leadership position is attained, the challenge becomes one of effectively functioning within the position and protecting, controlling, and retaining power. The questions then become, how do you balance political astuteness with personal values, professional integrity, and ethical standards? How do you develop an effective, efficient leadership style and still be an effective member of an existing leadership team with values different from yours? How do you achieve a balance between institutional goals and professional career goals?

Start immediately to develop and implement a strong, highly visible public image and professional public relations self-plan. Be highly visible on campus and in the community. Demonstrate genuine interest in the needs and concerns of institutional and community constituencies. Build an atmosphere of trust, empowering others to become creative, innovative contributors to common goals. Understand the institutional culture and mission and address issues aligned with overall institutional improvement and effectiveness.

Next, take every opportunity to practice and reflect upon leadership skills of communications, negotiations, analytical thinking, decision making, conflict resolution, political posturing, and analysis. Always wear the appropriate mask for the scene while on stage. Be genuine, but also be thoughtful, selective, and cautious. Remember, you did not get where you are without help; continually strengthen existing relationships and establish essential coalitions, alliances, networks, mentors, and confidants. Surround yourself not only with a strong, loyal administrative team, but also with people in powerful positions who may someday be helpful.

And finally, be competent and remain current in your professional field, in human relations, and about issues important to your institution and position.

Rule of Thumb
Blow your own horn regularly with gusto.
Maintain a highly visible, positive public persona.
Act like a winner.

Figure 4

Survival Manifesto for Women Administrators

1. The value of who you know far exceeds the value of what you know.
2. Be cautious and careful where you place your trust.
3. Never underestimate a competitor's ability to do you in.
4. Never let them see your pain; always maintain your composure.
5. Never reveal all of yourself to others; retain a level of mystery.
6. Never look surprised in public.
7. Know when to use power language.
8. Choose carefully what you get excited about.
9. Focus on one area at a time; diffusion of efforts creates confusion.
10. Face realities; it is possible to be terminated without just cause.

Source: Adapted from a speech delivered by A.J. Harrow and B.D. Holmes at the 1988 conference of the American Association of Community and Junior Colleges.

The Survival Manifesto in Figure 4 provides a declaration of political principles and intentions for women administrators.[26]

CONCLUSION

Peck opens his book, *The Road Less Traveled*, with the declaration that "life is difficult."[27] He contends that life is a series of problems which we are always in the process of confronting and solving; it is this very process of meeting and solving problems that brings meaning to life. His position is, one either moans about the problems or works out a plan to solve them. The latter requires self-discipline and skill.

Exclusion of women from important leadership positions in higher education is not a new problem, but rather one that has plagued American higher education for years and will continue to be a problem until women learn how to recognize, attain, and use power, and more actively support each other in "breaking through the glass ceiling." Now, as never before—with the strong national focus on restructuring higher education and the shifting power base nationally as well as world wide—is an opportune time for women to effectively work together formulating a strategic plan to ensure equity and diversity in higher education leadership opportunities.

Life is not fair; success is not equally distributed but fought for and won! In the words of Alinsky,

> "Political realists see the world as it is: an arena of
> power politics moved primarily by perceived immedi-
> ate self-interest, where morality is rhetorical rationale
> for expedient action and self-interest. It is a world not
> of angels but of angles, where men speak of moral
> principles but act on power principles."[28]

Women seeking high level leadership positions will continue to face challenges, but with the ability to assess the nature of power conflicts and analyze different contenders in the power struggles surrounding them, women will become more sophisticated competitors for leadership positions and be able to successfully cope with existing leadership styles until the time when higher education leaders recognize the value and contributions all members of the higher education family make.

The challenge, then, for women aspiring to serve as effective leaders in higher education in the coming century, is to establish strong knowledge and power bases, to build a strong web of support, and to come together as a force and apply "unrelenting legal and social pressure on all institutions to speed the pace of changing gatekeepers' attitudes about women in leadership roles.[29] As stated in the assumptions, no one can level the playing field alone nor will any group try until women in leadership positions today help pave the way for future women leaders by working as a strong team with an agenda to ensure there are opportunities for professional advancement beyond the "glass ceiling." It is time our voices are heard singing from the same sheet.

Betty Friedan states, "We must go from wallowing in the victim's state to mobilizing the new power of women and men for a larger political agenda on the priorities of life."[30]

Start now by applying these basic strategies for "crashing through those invisible barriers:"

- start promoting yourself in the right circles.
- take credit for your work and accomplishments.
- always remember you are dealing in an ever-changing, politically complex environment.
- create situations to associate with people and organizations powerful enough to make a difference in career advancement and survival.
- keep updated in your field and abreast of current issues affecting you and your institution.
- accept that analytical thinking and gamesmenship are essential to success.
- do something to make a difference.

Higher education leaders for the 21st Century face the challenges of meeting increased expectations of a more diverse population in a more complex, technological world with ever-decreasing resources. Competing in this changing, sophisticated, global society requires courageous leaders ready to accept and use power to promote and enhance growth and advancement opportunities for today's students and tomorrow's leaders. If as a society, we are to succeed in providing effective leadership for higher education in the 21st Century, we need to look beyond gender as a barrier to leadership positions, we need to provide equal opportunities for those prepared and willing to serve, and we need to develop an agenda for incorporating diversity within the higher education leadership structure.

While higher education administration has its difficult moments, it is challenging, rewarding, and commands the attention of competent women. There are many women leaders today ready and willing to meet this challenge. Women leaders of tomorrow are shaped in large measure by what we do today. We need to support each other and ensure leadership opportunities are made available for women now and in the future. We need a new voice for leadership in higher education; one which transcends male-dominated, power-oriented hierarchical institutional structures for leadership based upon ethical values and stressing empowerment and human development of the work force. We must forge ahead to strengthen higher education for the 21st Century.

ABSTRACT

The most difficult question posed by the metaphor in the title of this book, *Cracking the Wall*, is not whether or not there is a wall, but who is the architect of this wall, what is the nature of its construction, and is the wall real or an illusion?

ACE's *Factbook on Women in Higher Education* cites that women hold 11 percent of the highest administrative posts within institutions of higher education. Yet, women comprise about 34 percent of the pool of full-time managers and administrators in posts just below the top. This group, it would seem, might be in the promotional pool for the top slots in administration but there is considerable attrition in the final leap. No clear explanation exists as to why only 11 percent of this group makes it to the top or why 34 percent and not some larger percentage are in the promotional pool.

This chapter will explore some possible explanations and share, through the ideas of writers on empowerment, a potential dialogue. Organizing a discussion of empowerment literature in an attempt to state clearly what it says, is an overwhelming if not impossible task. It will be an imperfect dialogue. Nevertheless, it is necessary to begin somewhere. First, an attempt is made to explain what is meant by the term "empowerment." Second, an overview of empowerment literature as it affects women is presented. Finally, a dialogue is created which imagines an empowering conversation a woman may have with her inner self and others as she moves through key phases in the "walk" to the top post in higher education administration. Though this dialogue is necessarily asymmetrical, it is presented to capture the spirit of the literature, which is often instructive in a self-emancipating way.

Chapter Twelve

Empowerment:
The Politics of Change

Jean Treiman

Before I built a wall I'd ask to know
What I was walling in or walling out,
and to whom I was like to give offense.
Something there is that doesn't love a wall,
that wants it down.

Robert Frost
Mending Wall

*E*mpowerment is the politics of change. To seek empowerment is to seek change in traditionally held views of the fundamental controlling forces which shape our personal and social world. In *The Empowered Manager*, Peter Block defines empowerment in the organizational context as stemming from two sources: "(1) the structure, practices, and policies we support as managers who have control over others, and (2) the personal choices we make that are expressed by our own actions."[1] Eileen Bennet shares a personal view of empowerment for women, "Self-empowerment, the act of realizing and utilizing positive capacities of oneself such as autonomy, competency, creativity, self-esteem, and integrity, involves a woman on a journey to the authentic center of herself."[2]

JEAN ELIZABETH TREIMAN is a Research Fellow at the California Educational Research Cooperative, University of California in Riverside, California. She received her B.S. degree from California State University at Northridge; her M.A. degree from California Lutheran University and is expected to complete her Ph.D. in 1994 from the University of California, Riverside. Ms. Treiman's research areas are empowerment and women's issues in educational administration.

Most discussions of empowerment can be broadly categorized in two ways. The first is a formal public request for change requiring overt political action. In this context, the empowerment movement is seen as a necessary political tool used to gather an interest group and energize the forces necessary to make a public change or exchange between the "powers that be" and the "powers that want to be." The current professionalization movement in teaching might be characterized this way. In the second view, empowerment is a personal request for change. This is a self-transformation which seeks the incorporation of faculties or abilities not previously available or imagined. This view dominates most of the empowerment literature written by women, for women. Many articles, as Bennet explains, are essentially an attempt to have public conversations about things of a private nature involving self-permission and self-change.

Pervasive in the literature on empowerment, whether public transactions or personal transformations, is the idea of permanent change, change which requests a fundamental alteration of character for participants in the interaction. Placed in this context, it is easy to understand the barely suppressed excitement in empowerment literature which anticipates a change in traditions. Challenging personal and social traditions, whether mythical or real, requires tremendous energy, conviction, and self-examination.

Defining Empowerment

In an historical account of "Authority, Power and the Legitimation of Social Control," Douglas Mitchell and Bill Spady trace traditional views of power and authority in Western civilization. They propose that power and authority are two primary forces which are the founding concepts embedded in discussions of social control. These two forces are the substrata ideas of human experience which must be understood and accounted for in the study of social organization and change.[3] If this proposition is accepted at the outset, then the context of empowerment discussions can be placed within the sphere of conversations about conventionally held views of power and authority. The ancient Greeks used the term "dunamis" for power as "the ability to make things happen." The Greek view of authority, on the other hand, was action arising from "inner character" a kind of personal force used for the selection of a particular action. Since the notion of authority shaped the civilizing mission of the Romans and provided a link to an identification with a "transcendent national purpose," some believed the Roman view of authority was unique. The Romans expanded the concept of authority from a personal force to a collective cultural force.

Although hundreds of scholarly articles and books have been written to explain or critique classic Weberian views of the bureaucratization of power and authority in the Western world, there is little agreement about how these two mechanisms for control really work. In addition, in the past 20 years, there has been a considerable change in the usage of the term *authority*. Definitions used to involve such words as virtue, entrusted, right to act, and legitimate action.[4] Usage of the term has eroded and its meaning now reads more like a definition of power. Current references include such words as power to adjudicate, coercive power, power of rank, and power of sanction,[5] almost omitting the issue of legitimacy and trust as the uniquely human aspects of authority which Weber described.

Most recent discussions of power and authority in educational and organizational literature use the terms transactional forces and "transformational" forces instead of power and authority.[6] Transformation suggests an internal action or change of character used to alter a situation. This idea resembles earlier definitions of authority discussed by Mitchell and Spady. The term transactional force is often used to denote a power exchange or the change in an overt resource to alter a situation. Both are discussed as mechanisms for gaining social control, either personally or collectively.

Confusion about the definition of authority and its relationship to power hints at part of the crisis in empowerment discussions on the whole. If authority is thought of as legitimate control and is associated most often with a permitted and authorized agreement between two parties, then many of the empowerment queries can be seen as questions about legitimacy. Power, however, is the omnipresent "fill in the blank" term used to describe almost anything that is or seems like a force or a push. Terribly confused and misunderstood at this moment in Western culture, issues of social control are not made less confusing in discussions of empowerment.

It is hard to know, at times, who has what and how it got that way. Then, how can it be changed? There is a deceptively simple problem here. You can not change or alter something if you can not figure out what it is or wherein it resides. Empowerment literature questions allotments and endowments of power and authority. What kind of thinking, which cultural tradition, and which people have shaped authority and held power in the past, and why? A kind of "hunt" ensues in an attempt to find out where power and authority reside and what these ideas really mean. Then, when it is found, such as the notion of "position" within hierarchical control structures, even more complex questions evolve. It is from this basis of confusion, that empowerment literature attempts discussions about change.

Though this essay will not attempt to reconceptualize traditional notions of power and authority, it is probably important to remember that clarification would be useful.

What is clear in empowerment talk is the request for a permanent reauthorization and redistribution of the basic forces which shape society. Request for change is the single most emphatically clear idea in women's literature. Control issues typically discussed cover the political, professional, private and public rights of women—rights perceived as abridged or overlooked, in some way, perhaps by social injustice and stereotyping or by prior personal and cultural passivity. Perhaps the global nature of the request is an appropriate response to the sense of frustration expressed by scholars of women's issues.

At the end of a lecture on differences in cognition between men and women, Carol Jacklin, director of Women's Studies at the University of Southern California, explained, "research continues to demonstrate that no significant differences in thinking and cognitive patterns and processes exist between men and women. If differences exist, they appear to be a variable of cultural treatment and role expectation." An exasperated young woman raised her hand, "If that is so, then what can we do about this different treatment?" Carol laughed, "since we don't know what works, we simply must do everything!"[7]

Regardless of the changes sought, three themes recur which seem to define empowerment. The first is that of a reshaping of a personal force as if to provide an increase in potential energy, the second is a balancing of a social force which is perceived to be improperly balanced, and the third is the creation of a new political coalition in order to cause change in tradition. Interplay between these potential and dynamic forces for change is embedded in the literature.

When did Women Get into the Current Discussion

Empowerment of women is a national and international phenomena. Virginia Sapiro, in *The Political Integration of Women*, explains that its formal roots go back to the '60s when the women's movement grew in size and complexity.[8] In the last 10 years, thanks to the accumulated efforts of women's research centers and other academic groups interested in women's issues, hundreds of articles and books have been written on the issues of importance for women. Even though other groups, such as teachers and minorities, are discussed in empowerment literature, it would not be hard to conclude that "empowerment" is the best term for the real women's movement in the '90s.

American women want access to formal political power for different reasons than in the past. As fully enfranchised citizens of one of societies greatest democracies, they want power they sense is overdue and over-promised.

In addition, they want power in the work force which shapes their lives. Women are working, there is no sign that they are going home again, they are not helping out during a time of war, they are not just earning a second salary. Women find work important, necessary, and satisfying. They see work as a career and want formal recognition for their contribution to society. In this sense, current feminism is different from its earlier version in the '60s. Joanne Symons, Washington Public Affairs consultant, explains, "The new activist is not someone who says we need to take over political power, rather, they're saying, I'm trying to make a living, now it looks like I need political power to do that."[9]

A memory lingers, however, perhaps less understandable to the youngest generation of women in the work force, a memory of a generation of women who believed as youths that they and their male counterparts would see the "women's rights" revolution through. Now these women are asking, what happened? Current arguments are renewing a socially critical stance. Women's issues are not minority issues. Women are saying simply, we are one half of all beings born on the earth, we count and must be accounted for in the history of the world. As Symons points out in her commentaries, "women have found that legal equality has not produced social justice."[10] The current debate is often about issues of social justice. Richer in detail than ever before, academic discussions of social justice have developed a level of sophistication beyond self-conscious beginnings. This is testimony to earlier contributions which have created a knowledge base for women's studies and have produced an increased level of interest in the topic.

CURRENT CONVERSATIONS BETWEEN WOMEN AND MEN

There is a small window opening in the current conversations between men and women about empowerment. Women are no longer talking privately only to women, they are finding a new strength in a collective voice and public discourse between men and women. They are quicker to speak out, understanding the risks and not minding the wrath incurred in public debate. They are not walking away quietly when things go wrong.

New feminists are more self-reflective as there is a tiredness with the notion that "maleness" is somehow the root cause of the immorality and injustice inherent in our society. There is a need to recognize where women are, and to reinterpret the situation intellectually and rationally in order to make change. There is hope that a rational understanding and new research will illuminate human action and show the way.

But, role change is difficult. Do women lead men or do men lead women? Re-evaluating role perceptions is the nexus of the complex business of empowerment for women, particularly when the issue addresses top levels of political, positional, and hierarchical control at institutions such as colleges and universities.

In addition, real power isn't shared or given up easily. Sharon Kinsella cites one such fear, "Already, the economic pie is shrinking. Men are feeling threatened, like they're losing jobs to women as women become more aggressive in keeping their own place in the work force."[11] In, "Deference to Authority in the Feminized Professions," Linda Silver restates the age old Machiavellian notions of power.

In a society whose designation as a "man's world" is only now in some dispute, it is not surprising that organizations defined and controlled by men should relegate women to subordinate statuses. Privilege, whether absolute or relative, is rarely shared willingly.[12]

Silver raises an ancient flag signalling the optimistic rationalists, that an irrational battle of multiple excuses rather than multiple intelligence may await women who move to the top.

Since so few women hold the top posts in organizational hierarchies, there is little cultural evidence of successful experience. Whether arguments at the top are rational or irrational is hard to know. Issues of power, privilege, and male domination are difficult to study. Sensitive questions need to be asked about hiring practices in a highly secretive and highly ritualized world.

If women had top positional power would they exercise it in the same way men do? In *The Feminization of America*, Barbara Myeroff and Eleanor Lenz point out that women act quite different from men in the board room. They argue that women bring a unique view of power and authority and that this caring, feminized, and desperately needed perspective is necessary to humanize the workplace.[13] How women might affect changes in organizational cultures at the top is largely unknown. In a democracy which has not experienced a female president, and with 2 percent of the United States Senate and 6 percent of the House of Representatives being women, working role models are hard to find.[14] There are few women CEOs in the nation's major corporations so there is simply insufficient information available about the way women exercise power and authority in top posts.

Is there anger and backlash against women who pursue empowerment and change? Along with concerns for more proportionate representation in society's important institutions, there is a re-emergence of concern for the erosion of women's personal and political rights. Hate crimes against women are on the rise and many women are concerned about backlash in the workplace.[15] Nevertheless, new battles will be shaped differently from the past. Few observers would disagree that women have "outed" into the public world in a different way from the past, and though the current conversations sound more like a call to speed up an evolution, rather than a call to a revolution, it is likely that memories and experiences from the '60s have helped.

LITERATURE ON EMPOWERMENT IN DIFFERENT DISCIPLINES

Empowerment is a multifaceted, complex topic which is fuzzy and overlapping. Discussions can perhaps be compared to an auto-focus zoom lens that can't decide which object ought to be in clear view. Articles sometimes appear to critique a small issue in one tiny corner of the world and, simultaneously to critique the very fabric of social organization in the Western world.

Psychological and Physical Empowerment

Searching through psychological literature is painful. So many articles focus on the psychological and physical empowerment necessary for women to overcome victimization. Rape and other forms of physical and mental abuse of women provide a solemn reminder that acts of aggression uncover a thin veil of civility and a great deal of anger which is condoned by society. Though not within the scope of this discussion, unchecked physical aggression and violence has led many women's study researchers to view the "privatization" of women's lives as a fundamental social mechanism for keeping unwanted acts of abuse from the public eye.[16] More women understand now that there is a clear difference between matters of intimacy, which are related to private, personal and family life, and matters of "privatization" which suggest an inappropriate suppression of the business of women's lives with an attendant gain in power to the oppressor. The road to self-repair caused by unwanted acts of male aggression is long and arduous. Public disclosure is still risky for women and justice elusive. What seems most important to understand is that knowledge of certain pain can suppress open conversation. Victimization is a feeling in the air, and like a disease can spread in the imagination of women's minds as they attempt to construct conversations with themselves about the consequences of self-assertion. Private thoughts which might become public actions come with "cost" and benefits must be imagined to outweigh. Jean Bethke Elshtain's, *Public Man, Private Women*, provides a historical discussion of the roots of the private lives of women. She devotes the final chapter to suggestions for the reconstruction of the private and public lives of men and women to provide more symmetry in relationships.[17]

Sociological Empowerment

Sociological literature on empowerment in the work force provides a basis for understanding and documenting the changes in the public spheres as women exercise increasing influence in the workplace. In her book, *Politics and Sexual Equality*, Pippa Norris provides a detailed empirical study of the current economic and social status of women, and the current sexual stratification of women in Western society.[18]

The Feminization of America provides a discussion of changes occurring in board rooms and workplaces as women bring their contributions to the table. An optimistic but thoughtful dialogue, it provides a balance to current more critical views of social organizations by discussing ways in which men benefit and society-at-large benefits from points of view distinctly held by women. Lenz and Myeroff document patterns of interaction which are changing decision making processes and leadership actions in social organizations.

Educational and Professional Empowerment

Educational literature on empowerment concentrates on formal changes in the distribution of power and authority among teachers, parents, and site level managers. Universally in Western Civilization teachers are seeking greater control and responsibility for professional decision making. With an increased sense of professionalism, they seek to give meaningful input which will not only be heard, but be acted upon to exercise real control over the workplace. Interestingly, much of the dialogue in teacher empowerment involves shared decision making and a democratization of the workplace. In *Restructuring Schools to Empower Teachers*, Bruce Romanish captures the essence of teacher empowerment, "When teachers are empowered, they will have authorization to significantly influence and participate in decisions related to the educational undertaking in virtually all its dimensions...to have power in its true sense means there is no need for it to be "allowed."[19] Peeling back a thin layer of this dialogue reveals a somewhat covert discussion between administrators, mostly males, and teachers, mostly females. The tenor of this dialogue does not differ from Amatai Etzioni's discussions about feminized and socially devalued occupations such as teaching, librarianships, and nursing. Recently, women have chosen teaching as a career and have done so with an awakened understanding of professional rights and responsibilities. They are beginning to embrace the political implications of this form of empowerment.

Organizational Empowerment and Women

Organizational empowerment literature revolves around two themes: conceptions of management style, and demystification and participation in the structuration of modern organizations.

In *Educational Administration Quarterly*, Dunlap and Goldman discuss power as a system of "facilitation" rather than a force for social control.[20] Within this discussion is a subtopic which could be labeled "participatory management" or "shared decision making" styles. These styles often appear in discussions of organizational control which are associated with feminine ways of dealing with power.

Organizational literacy is important to women. Women have less formal knowledge and experience with the macro-structures of orga-

nizations and certainly no experience in designing them. In an analysis of the mystification of organizational structures, R.J.S. "Mac" MacPherson discusses intentional use of organizationally unique "structuration" to mystify "outsiders" and preserve the stability of the inner leadership group. Prior to formal meetings, organizational cultures maintain control of agenda and issues by informal conversations and corridor talk designed to facilitate political agreements and consensus building. Women are seldom found in the "inner arena" and the "corridors" and hence have a hard time exercising influence over organizational agendas. Preservation of structuration, that is the creation and control of knowledge about being organized, works to preserve the status quo.[21]

Empowered Leadership and Women

Empowered leadership is a plaintive dialogue between subordinates and leaders. Block's *Empowered Manager*, is one such dialogue. Leaders are requested to recognize and respond to persistent complaints about restrictive and thoughtless control, rigid bureaucracies, dehumanizing institutions, and top-down rule-making. Empowered managers are expected to release subordinates from "patriarchal contracts" and encourage workers to be their own authority, able to express themselves, make commitments and believe in the just request for such power. Block suggests turning the organizational triangle upside down with the broader bottom of the pyramid at the top and the point resting at the base, to illustrate the idea of the empowered worker.[22]

Women are generally adept at the "bottom-up" acquisitions of power and feel comfortable with undefined, informal authority. Carol Shakeshaft notes in her research on empowerment and educational leadership that women are "more likely to empower others and work collaboratively to achieve group goals."

Recent conversations about leadership have been more balanced and less accusing of leaders who earn legitimate authority and attempt to exercise control over organizations. John Mitchell's recent work, *Re-Visioning Educational Leadership*, asks administrators to revisit the idea of legitimated leadership and its relationship to organizational control.[23] Balance is essential to a realization that an organizational community is particularly vulnerable to counterproductive turbulence if a core vision is not held and preserved by leaders who guide followers. Leaders are empowered to transform the organizational vision into a mission. Empowered leaders are people whose values and character involve a deep regard for the transformational nature of the organizational enterprise and the intrinsic rewards of a caring, self-reconstructing, well functioning workplace.

Shakeshaft adds that issues of equity ought to be at the central core of this vision and suggests that colleges and universities who teach leadership need to model this vision in their own programs.[24]

Empowerment of Women in Higher Education Administration

An assumption is made at the outset of this section that the top post in an institution of higher education is a formal political post. To think otherwise would be naive at best. Institutions, which are the chief knowledge production and legitimating agencies for our culture delegate raw political power to their executives. They have the opportunity to decide what knowledge is legitimate, which research questions get funded and are therefore seen as significant. They plan and execute training programs for the intellectual elite of our culture. Politically and culturally top administrators are very powerful.

Not surprisingly, some of the best articles about women and higher education administration are found in smaller journals such as *Initiatives* and the *School Library Journal*. There are accounts of personal success stories, attempts to warn women about the political nature of the last rung of the hierarchical ladder, as well as empirical reminders that when women do get to the top they feel more stress and they feel it differently from men. As Flora Ortiz suggests in her research on educational administration, not much is found in mainstream journals on women's issues and issues of sex equity.[25] It would appear barriers are still operating to keep discussions out of the mainstream.

The wall of greatest significance in a move on to the top posts in higher education may well be the "political wall." As Virginia Sapiro points out, "*Women* don't belong in politics."[26] Positions of political influence involve daily decisions about primary power resources. Social taboos and myths abound when women are seen as power wielders and politicians. Women are experts at "second degree" power that is delegated power and support roles, like management. A woman must have complex conversations with herself and others in order to see survival in the formal political role essential in top positions.

AN IMPERFECT DIALOGUE

In a recent article on teacher empowerment, Richard Prawatt[27] presents a thoughtful framework for conversations with "self and others" which guides a reflective discussion of personal empowerment. What follows here is an attempt to imagine a conversation with "inner self and others" as women move to the top. A transitional walk from private to public life, and from professional to political life is presented.

The path imagined here is not presented as one woman's path, but is a reference point. To the extent that one can collect and envision such experiences, this conversation might be a useful mechanism for generalizing about collective experiences.

CONVERSATION WITH SELF: PRIVATE LIFE TO PUBLIC LIFE

Something there is that doesn't love a wall,
that wants it down. I could say 'Elves' to him,
but it's not elves exactly, and I'd rather
He said it for himself.

"Mending Wall" provides a thoughtful beginning for the self-enabling conversations women must go through as they leave their private world and go to work.[28] Many doubts and fears must be reconciled and overcome before one can proceed. It is in this way that we must walk "through the walls" of our personal construction to sort out what is real and what is illusion. The sheer volume of research on the private lives of women is almost oppressive, but what is apparent even to the casual reader is that there is much to say. From birth men are expected to go to work in the public world. They prepare for this all of their lives. A woman must prepare for this differently. She must prepare the family for her leaving, she must envision her success in both the entry into the work force and the re-entry to the home. She must envision how others in her life will understand her decision to work. She must weigh the contribution it will make to the family and home. No great external social force is lined up to see her succeed. She must imagine a retreat if the family is threatened. She may imagine herself selfish in this pursuit if it is seen by others as unnecessary or injurious to the family health. She must weigh the duplicity of the walk with conversations about what could go wrong during her absence and what is contributed to the family by entrance into public life. She must weigh these arguments against time honored traditions of the derived social self-worth of women as homemakers.

Though it has changed in recent debates, the topic of self-emancipation is the oldest argument on the shelf of feminine literature. Nevertheless, conversations with self and the granting of permission to enter the work force is still a formidable task for women. This is especially true now that an open public debate rages about the problems of fractured family life in America. Who is to blame? Society looks for scapegoats. After 30 years of feverish discussion about women's roles in society, a woman's primary sense of self-worth as prescribed by her prewritten social contract and her own needs for love and approval is still derived from seeing to the needs of family. She is to be first "relational," then rational in her constructed conversations. Other people first, self second, and outer achievements third.

Though women today feel this is not the only measure of self-worth available to them, few would argue that home and family, home and caring, home and privacy are not concepts associated with womanhood. A woman may ask herself what happens if she denigrates this personal power, what will replace it? Home is the hallowed societal institution for which she has primary responsibility. Even ardent feminists are recanting about the immeasurable satisfactions of good home life.

But, meshing homeworld and workworld is her problem. Little has changed within social institutions to assist her with this task. At work, if she is part time, she is less committed and less likely to receive advancement. If she is full time she is still expected to be home with sick children but not to miss work. She keeps the family appointments and commitments, albeit after work. She imagines solutions to many scenarios as she becomes committed to two roles which are demanding and often incompatible. If she fails at "homemaking" as she steps into the public world, she will live with that failure on a minute by minute basis until this shame is resolved.

If she is divorced, she will balance the books whether the child support comes or not, much of the time, not. She will work in a lesser paid job, have less time off and find herself to blame if something goes wrong with the kids. The stress of the family is hers, it follows wherever she goes.

Where does this conversation end—it sounds so unfair? As Elshtain explains in her essay on reconstructing public and private worlds of women, the work problem comes to "a central kind of fizzle called false promises." As women have entered the world of work they simply find "homework" waiting when they return. Much has been discussed between men and women about sharing the chores of family life, but real progress is hard to see.

Make no mistake, empirical research suggests that women in high positions in administration share the same family stresses as do women who are secretaries. In addition, their jobs often require spur of the moment travel and job tasks which reach well beyond the hours of the local day care center or the time when "caring" women are expected at home. The myth a woman must live up to is a deep seated understanding that "men don't wreck homes, women do."[29]

As a woman stands at the family doorstep, leaving a perplexed family and nation facing itself...she asks herself not what am I doing *for* my family but what am I doing *to* my family as I go to work.

CAREER CHOOSING

A man's career does not center around a "fit" with the maintenance of home. Choosing a worthy career and preparing for it, is a joint societal task. Often parents, family and society stand ready to make sacrifices to see that he becomes a "bread winner." Even though this is a formidable challenge for the male in our society, he is not risking family to do it. Just the opposite, he is expected to do this for the "sake" of family. Society provides no such extended or ready support for women. Privatization, no more!

At another level, the "privatization" of women's lives is an empowerment argument which suggests that the social constraints of staying at home have deprived women of a public ear for problems which should concern society.

Women find a kind of "democratic harbor" in the public workplace and they are leaving the door open at home and taking the democratization and the expectations of equity in the work force home with them. Feminists such as Sharon Kinsella have always preached the "private and personal-is-political" message, both in the work force and at home. In an interview, she explains she is finding a more receptive audience as women share private fears and problems with others at work.[30] Public work allows control over a life made vulnerable to exploitation and alienation.

New reflections are in the mirror. Images of self are not only formed by family. Exercises of natural, charismatic and relational influence emerge in the social settings along with intellectual influence. An important transformation happens as work becomes a career. In the past, home life may have been a barrier to work simply because it was "there" it was accepted as a woman's own "lived situation." Work in the outside world has brought "possibility" into women's lives and given them some control over their lives in ways not previously imagined. In this simple way perhaps things are different forever.

ACADEMIC CAREERS: TWO PATHS AND LATE ARRIVALS

Two paths toward a career in higher education are typical for women. The first is a choice driven by thinking of oneself as "biologist" and a member of a special academic community, the second is choosing a "semi-profession" or "feminized profession" such as teaching or librarianship and then selecting a college or university career.

Research suggests conversations with "self as professional" may differ for young women who finish a Ph.D. program in a more "male typical" time frame. Men finish six to nine years earlier than the average women.[31] Conversations with "self as professional" by women who have consciously joined what is called a "semi-profession" or "feminized profession" without prior experience in higher education are more difficult. Late arrival is a problem as is visualization of success in a non-homemaker compatible job. An alteration of family expectations may be necessary.

CONVERSATIONS WITH SELF: PROFESSIONAL LIFE TO POLITICAL LIFE

Thinking of self as a fully enfranchised professional requires attention to the regulation and constitution of the professional community. It is here that the experience of committee work and an early initiation into the politics of professional governance are made. This step is an important first step into formal politics of the college and university organization.

Developing conversations with self as expert among peers of equal relationship and influence does not appear to be a problem or a barrier for women. However, professional empowerment continues as participation in the scholarly community revolves around career development and successful networking. Participation in key "fast track" type experiences which are seen to assist promotion in the administrative world requires mentorship. Women who are mentored build the confidence to succeed.

But, expert authority and prior administrative experience is not the only prerequisite to move to the top.

Am I a Politician?

Elves may warn and whisper in a woman's ear, "You want to be on top? Things are different here, things are different here."

> People often call university administrators bureaucrats, implying that they are red-tape specialists, but that is a childishly naive understanding of our role. Sure, there are indeed lower-level administrators who are paper pushers and bureaucrats in the old sense of the work, but the men in the critical roles are not bureaucrats, they are politicians, struggling to make dreams come true and fighting to balance interests groups off against each other. This place is more like a political jungle, alive and screaming, than a rigid, quiet bureaucracy.

A senior administrator at N.Y.U.[32]

The difference here is politics. As this senior administrator so perfectly reveals, only masculine pronouns need apply. No conversation in a woman's personal history is an adequate rehearsal for the constant and often painful arguments with self and others which lie ahead as a woman steps into the positional, political power hierarchy of administration. Friends will see her differently and she will see herself differently.

A conversation might start as youthful as, Mother, may I take "one giant step" into a world beyond your imagining, a world that is foreign to you, a world where taboos abound, a risky world where I can not imagine myself succeeding as there is little history there, there is only future. I whisper the words...I want to be president of this college. I secretly rehearse these and other strange sounding conversations. Everything seems secret now...I risk conversation only with myself.

REPOSITIONING THE POLITICAL SELF WITH OTHERS

The political wall, by simple empirical evidence, is substantial. The top path is a formal political path. Much evidence suggests that this is the thickest wall; a woman's imagining and no illusions will assist her in clearing the hurdle.

Women are not only politically inexperienced and often lack formal education to assist them with this journey, but other impedances surface to haunt them. The risks required to be successful in a political post at a college or university may cause conflict within the very character of their being.

Moving up to a position of power in the first degree requires an alteration in the facilitative and relational exercises of power and authority, which made work with peers productive in the past. The gentle permissive authority of professional expertise seems like a distant conversation when women look in the mirror and find a "powerbroker."

A first degree power leap may feel more like being propelled through space with a primal scream. The conversation? Do women belong here? I don't see many. Is this really a man's world, isn't there some natural law, some territorial imperative I am breaking? Will my mentors and friends think less of me?

Women are experts at second degree power, they are used to assisting and servicing others with minimal resources and delegated or derived authority. Women know they are good at this. Mitchell describes these modes of social control as displacement modes, indirect and permissive, derived from the two direct mechanisms of social control defined as power and authority. Far back in the history of Western tradition, public acts of power and authority have been exercised by men. Direct control over allocation of resources and hiring and firing workers are not typical experiences for women. The "powerbroker" in the mirror may have deferred to "higher authority" in the past, an action no longer possible now.

A whole host of accusers may be in the mirror, including self, as a new positional vision is shaped. In the *Political Integration of Women*, Sapiro captures the discontinuity perfectly.

Politics and women. For most people at most times these two words have harmonized neither on paper nor in the mind. They are cacophonous words, contradictory terms. Together they call up amusing pictures, Nast-like images of cigar-smoking women in crinolines. Just as often this vision is a nightmare: "The conclusive objection to the political franchise of women is, that it would weaken and finally break up and destroy the Christian family..." Increasing involvement of women in political life has been blamed for the spread of a wide range of 'social evils'...[33]

The reconnective moment in this dialogue goes back to the first conversation...is the public, political woman-self able to have an integrated conversation with the personal, relational woman-self. Are these two selves filled with competing value systems requiring a compromise of one's character to move from one sphere to the other. Is bifurcation necessary? When women make personal passions into public arguments, it is necessary to transition from private spheres of influence to political spheres. They make themselves vulnerable to an asymmetry associated with socially normed expectations that women don't yield power, men do.

The asymmetry in this conversation is nested around gender differentiation and socialization arguments as to who should rightly exercise and manipulate direct power and authority over others in the public world and in social institutions.

In addition to integrating private and political self, a problem occurs when women, often having nothing other than male mentorship in higher positions, attempt to emulate men and find out different things happen when they do. The exercise of power for women has a different set of social rules.

Rebuke for the use of a tactic associated with males, for example, an assertive attempt to take control of a meeting in order to get work done, may come as much from within the self as from others. Yet, a more feminine tactic, such as seeking consensus, may be misunderstood as weakness even if results are the same. Often a woman may feel she is in a lose-lose situation. If I take on male tactics, I'm accused of manlike behavior, unfeminine...if I am feminine I am weak and may not be doing my job.

In higher education administration socially normed behavior is male; in politics, socially normed behavior is male; and exercises of rational and traditional authority are associated with maleness. Until these social stereotypes are set aside, excuses and explanations may replace reason.

CONCLUDING THOUGHTS: WHO IS GUILTY?

A woman's path to a top level post of the most hallowed, traditional, authoritative place in the intellectual world, is no doubt a unique one. Conversations are fraught with disillusionment, mystery, misunderstanding and a sense of betrayal. They turn to whispers when women share intimate pain, stories are told of silent footsteps as leave takings, turning of backs and a quiet tip-toeing away into the darkness of vague things behind the wall.

Tearing down the "political walls" which are barriers to the full participation of women in society requires joint effort and understanding. However uncomfortable on-going discussions of empowerment may be, it seems imperative to rethink issues in order to shape justified changes in the formal power and authority arrangements in social institutions.

One final hurdle, Sapiro suggests, is that scholars who want to study political problems facing women in our culture, are often viewed as "shrill," "polemical," or "irrational." This is the scholarly myth which must be torn down in order to shed new light on real issues.

Maybe the 1990s will be a time of new partnerships.

> *Something there is that doesn't love a wall,*
> *That sends the frozen-ground-swell under it,*
> *And spills the upper boulders in the sun;*
> *And makes gaps even two can pass abreast.*

> Robert Frost[36]
> *Mending Wall*

Postscript

John P. Schlegel

Susan Faludi in her recent book *Backlash* notes that by the end of the decade of the 1980s "women were starting to tell pollsters that they feared their social status was once again beginning to slip. They believed they were facing an 'erosion of respect'."[1] Can that same observation be applied to the role of women in higher education administration?

This monograph has provided some salient observations regarding factors that have prevented women from preparation for successful entry into senior level administrative positions in higher education. To be sure, many women administrators have beaten the odds and have broken through the glass ceiling—that transparent barrier that keeps women from rising above a certain level. However, they too, with all of their success continue to face obstacles to their professional development.

Without a doubt, the number of women in significant administrative positions is increasing, yet they remain underrepresented. At a time when women are a majority in our nation, when women constitute more than half of the students enrolled in America's colleges and universities, and women are claiming a greater role in politics, it is asserted that only 11 percent of the chief executive officers in our institutions of higher education in 1989 were women. While a larger

JOHN P. SCHLEGEL, S.S. is President of the University of San Francisco. He has served as Executive and Academic Vice President at John Carroll University. He has been the Dean of Arts and Sciences at Marquette University and Rockhurst College, and an Assistant Academic Vice President and Associate Professor in the Department of Political Science at Creighton University. He is a trustee of various high schools and universities including Loyola University of Chicago and Loyola College, Maryland. He is active in accreditation activities and has served as a consultant to various economic and arts and humanities commissions. He has been an American Council on Education Fellow, Visiting Research Scholar at the University of Ottawa and has been a Fellow and Research Associate at the Commonwealth Institute, Oxford University. He has published in the area of comparative politics and International Relations. He holds a B.A. in Philosophy and Classics and an M.A. in Political Science from St. Louis University; a B.D. in Theology from the University of London, and a D.Phil. in International Relations from Oxford University.

number of women administrators were clustered at the lowest level of administration. At the same time, the literature reports that women in higher education administration continue to trail behind their male counterparts in pay and promotion. The same allegation is made concerning women in the ranks of faculty.

There is an irony in this situation. If higher education is truly to be proactive with respect to social change, if higher education is to instill in its students both social and ethical patterns for leading productive and responsible lives, then these same institutions should be at the forefront of equity issues; the role of women in the academy being one of the most significant issues of equity. At a time in American higher education when many institutions are concerned with issues of diversity and multicultural representation, there should be an equal commitment to gender balance in the hiring, promotion, and retention of administrators and faculty alike.

As we look towards the end of our decade, higher education is a troubled profession. Both state supported and private institutions are faced with worsening economic conditions, spiraling costs, and a declining public confidence in higher education and the value of its product. Faced with the uncertainties of the future, we are in no position to discount or discredit the valuable resources present in the many women professionals entering or already present in our ranks. We need to look beyond gender as a barrier to leadership positions; we need to provide equal opportunities for those prepared and willing to serve; we need to develop an agenda for incorporating gender diversity within the higher education leadership structure. The same opportunities for mentoring, networking, and improvement that were available to my generation of male administrators must be made accessible for women.

1. Susan Faludi, *Backlash*, p. 18.

References

Chapter 1. Career Paths of Women in Higher Education

1. R.M. Heming, "Women In Community College Administration: A Progress Report." *Journal of the National Association of Women Deans, Administrators, and Counselors.* 46 (1985) 3-8. Kathryn M. Moore, "Careers in College and University Administration: How Are Women Affected?" *New Directions for Higher Education.* 45 (1984) 5-15. Adrian Tinsley, "Upward Mobility for Women Administrators." *Journal of the National Association of Women Deans, Administrators, and Counselors.* 49 (1985) 3-11. National Association of State Universities and Land-Grant Colleges. 1989. *Assessing Change.* Washington, D.C. American Council on Education, "Number of Women Presidents Doubles Since 1975." *Higher Education and National Affairs,* 39 (1990) 1-4.

2. ACE, *Higher Education and National Affairs,* 1990.

3. Solomon Polachek, "Occupational Segregation Among Women: Theory, Evidence, and a Prognosis," in *Women in the Labor Market,* Cynthia Lloyd (ed.) (New York: Columbia University Press, 1979), 137-157. Solomon Polachek, "Occupational Self-Selection: A Human Capital Approach to Sex Differences in Occupational Structure." *Review of Economics and Statistics,* 58 (1981) 60-69.

4. Solomon Polachek, "Women in the Economy: Perspectives on Gender Inequality," in *Comparable Worth: Issues for the 80s: A Consultation of the U.S. Commission on Civil Rights,* edited by the U.S. Commission on Civil Rights, Washington D.C.: U.S. Government Printing Office.

5. Rachel A. Rosenfeld and Jo Ann Jones, "Patterns and Effects of Geographic Mobility for Academic Women and Men." *Journal of Higher Education,* 58 (1987) 494-515.

6. Moore, *New Directions for Higher Education,* 1984. Rosabeth M. Kanter, "Men and Women of the Corporation." (New York: Harper and Row, 1977).

7. Laurel Richardson, "The Dynamics of Sex and Gender: A Sociological Perspective." Third Edition (1988). Patricia A. Roos and Barbara R. Reskin, "Institutional Factors Contributing to Sex Segregation in the Workplace," in *Sex Segregation in the Workplace,* (Washington D.C.: National Academy Press, 1984).

8. Kathryn N. Moore and M.A. Sagaria, "Women Administrators and Mobility: The Second Struggle." *Journal of the National Association of Women Deans, Administrators, and Counselors,* 44 (1981) 21-28. Kathryn Moore, Ann Salimbene, Joyce Marlier and Stephen Bragg, "The Structure of Presidents' and Deans' Careers." *Journal of Higher Education,* 54 (1983) 500-515.

9. Henry Rosovksy, "Deaning." *Harvard Magazine,* January-February (1987) 34-40. Bernice Sandler, "The Campus Climate Revisited: Chilly for Women Faculty, Administrators, and Graduate Students." Project of the Status and Education of Women. (Washington D.C.: Association of American Colleges, 1986).

10. Paula England, George Farkas, Thomas Dou, and Barbara Kilbourne, "Explaining Occupational Sex Segregation and Wages: Findings from a Model with Fixed Effects." *American Sociological Review,* 53 (1988) 544-558. Roos and Reskin, *Sex Segregation in the Workplace,* 1984.

11. Robert P. Althauser and Arne L. Kalleberg, "Firms, Occupations, and the Structure of Labor Markets: A Conceptual Analysis." *Sociological Perspectives on Labor Markets,* Ivar Berg (ed.) (New York: Academic Press, 1981).

12. Roos and Reskin, 1984.

13. Tinsley, 1985.

14. Simon Langlois, "Les Reseaux Personnels et la Diffusion des Informations Sur Les Emplois." *Recherches Sociographiques,* 2 (1977) 213-245. Mark S. Granovetter, *Getting a Job: A Study of Contact and Careers.* Cambridge, MA: Harvard University Press (1974). Shirley M. Clark and Mary Corcoran, "Perspectives on the Professional Socialization of Women Faculty." *Journal of Higher Education,* 57 (1986) 20-43.

15. Raymond Noe, "Women and Mentoring: A Review and Research Agenda." *Academy of Management Review,* 13 (1988) 65-78. Seymour Spilerman, "Careers, Labor Market Structure, and Socioeconomic Achievement." *American Journal of Sociology,* 83 (1978) 551-593. Elizabeth J. McNeer, "Two Opportunities for Mentoring: A Study of Women's Career Development in Higher Education Administration." *Journal of the National Association of Women Deans, Administrators, and Counselors,* 47 (1983) 8-14.

16. Moore, 1984. Carol Shakeshaft, *Women in Educational Administration,* (Beverly Hills, CA: Sage Publications, 1987).

17. England, et al., 1988.

18. Tinsley, 1985.

19. Moore and Sagaria, 1981.

20. Cynthia Secor, "Preparing the Individual for Institutional Leadership: The Summer Institute." Donna Shavlik and Judith G. Touchton, "Toward a New Era of Leadership: The National Identification Program," in *Women in Higher Administration,* Adrian Tinsley, Cynthia Secor and Sheila Kaplan (eds.). (San Francisco, CA: Jossey-Bass, 1984).

Chapter 4. Barriers to Women's Advancement

1. Nadya Aisenberg and Mona Harrington, *Women of Academe: Outsiders in the Sacred Grove,* (Amherst: University of Massachusetts Press, 1988), 3.

2. Bryan Wilson, *Education, Education & Society*, (New York: Harper & Row Publishers, 1975), 9.

3. Ibid.

4. Jean Bethke Elshtain, *Public Man, Private Woman*, (Princeton: Princeton University Press, 1981).

5. Ibid.

6. Ibid.

7. Aisenberg and Harrington, *Women of Academe*, 4.

8. Ibid., 4-5.

9. Charles N. Halaby, "Sexual Inequality in the Workplace: An Employer-Specific Analysis of Pay Differences," *Social Science Research*, 8 (1979), 79-104.

10. William Bielby and James N. Baron, "A Woman's Place is with Other Women: Sex Segregation Within Organizations," in *Sex Segregation in the Workplace: Trends, Explanations, Remedies*, Barbara F. Reskin, (ed.). (Washington, D.C.: National Academy Press, 1984), 27-55.

11. Robert E. Szafran, *University and Women Faculty: Why Some Organizations Discriminate More Than Others*, (New York: Praeger, 1984), 5-7.

12. Alison M. Konrad and Jeffrey Pfeffer, "Understanding the Hiring of Women and Minorities in Educational Institutions," *Sociology of Education*, (1991), Vol. 64 (July), 141-157.

13. Ibid., 143.

14. Book of Proverbs, 23:7.

15. Konrad and Pfeffer, 141-152.

16. Tillie Olsen, *Silences*, (New York: Delacorte, 1978).

17. A.R. Hoschschild, "Inside the Clockwork of Male Careers," in *Women and the Power to Change*, F. Howe, (ed.). (New York: McGraw-Hill, 1975), 49.

18. Ibid.

19. Lynne B. Welsch, *Women in Higher Education: Changes and Challenges*, (New York: Praeger, 1990), 9.

20. William R. Brown, *Academic Politics*, (Alabama: The University of Alabama Press, 1982), 103.

21. Rita J. Wolotkiewicz, *College Administrator's Handbook*, (Boston: Allyn and Bacon, Inc., 1980), 15.

22. Ibid.

23. Myra Per-Lee, Vice-President of Enrollment Management, National University. Interview with author, San Diego, CA: October 16, 1991.

24. Myra Per-Lee, Interview.

25. Russell Edgerton, *Expanding Faculty Options: Career Development Projects at Colleges and Universities*, (AAHE, Washington, D.C., 1981), 1-2.

26. Ibid., 67.

27. Myra Per-Lee, Interview.

Chapter 5. **Redesigning the Ivory Tower**

1. Ann Fuehrer and Karen Maitland Schilling, "The Values of Academe: Sexism as a Natural Consequence," *Journal of Social Issues* 41 (1985) (4), 29-42. Judith G. Touchton and Lynne Davis, *Fact Book on Women in Higher Education*, (New York: American Council on Education and Macmillan, 1991). Carola Eisenberg, "Affirmative Action for Women and Promotion of Academic Excellence," *Academic Medicine* 66 (November, 1991), 678-79.

2. Fueher and Schilling, 29-42. Bradley Googins and Dianne Burden, "Vulnerability of Working Parents: Balancing Work and Home Roles," *Social Work* 32 (July/August, 1987), 295-300. Arthur G. Bedeian, Beverly G. Burke, & Richard G. Moffett, "Outcomes of Work-family Conflict Among Married Male and Female Professionals," *Journal of Management* 14 1988 (3), 475-91. Laraine T. Zappert and Harvey M. Weinstein, "Sex Differences in the Impact of Work on Physical and Psychological Health," *American Journal of Psychiatry* 142 (October, 1985), 1174-78.

3. Janice D. Yoder, "An Academic Woman as a Token: A Case Study," *Journal of Social Issues* 41 1985 (4), 61-72. Fuehrer and Schilling, 29-42. Carol C. Nadelson, "Professional Issues for Women," *Women's Disorders* 12 (March, 1989), 25-33. Dana E. Friedman, *Family-supportive Policies: The Corporate Decision-making Process.* (New York: Conference Board, 1987). Report No. 897.

4. United States Department of Labor Women's Bureau. *Working Mothers and their Children.* (Washington, D.C.: U.S. Government Printing Office, 1989). (Publication No. 0-248-962: QL 3).

5. B.J. Biddle, "Recent Developments in Role Theory," *Annual Review of Sociology* 12 1986, 67-92.

6. Paula M. Popovich and Betty Jo Licata, "A Role Model Approach to Sexual Harassment," *Journal of Management* 13 (1987)(1), 149-61.

7. Marcia Killien and Marie Annette Brown, "Work and Family Roles of Women: Sources of Stress and Coping Strategies. *Health Care for Women International* 8 (2-3), 169-84.

8. Elaine M. Brody, "Women in the Middle," *The Gerontologist* 21 (1981)(5), 471-80. Bilha Mannheim and Meira Schiffrin, "Family Structure, Job Characteristics, Rewards and Strains as Related to Work-role Centrality of Employed and Self-employed Professional Women with Children," *Journal of Occupational Behavior* 5: (1984), 83-101.

9. Felice Schwartz, "Management Women and the New Facts of Life," *Harvard Business Review* 89 (January-February, 1989), 65-76.

10. Catherine D. Gaddy, Carol R. Glass, and Diane B. Arnkoff, "Career Involvement of Women in Dual-career Families: The Influence of Sex Role Identity," *Journal of Counseling Psychology* 30 (3) (1983), 388-94.

11. Googins and Burden, 1987.

12. Sara Yogev, "Are Professional Women Overworked? Objective Versus Subjective Perception of Role Loads," *Journal of Occupational Psychology* 55 (3) (1982), 165-69.

13. Brody, 1981. Michael A. Creedon, "Introduction," in *Issues for an Aging America: Elder Care* (Report No. 911), Dana E. Friedman, (ed.), 2-3. (New York: Conference Board, 1988). Robyn Stone, Gail Lee Cafferata, and Judith Sangl, "Caregivers of the Frail Elderly: A National Profile," *The Gerontologist* 27 (1987) (5), 616-26. Janice L. Gibeau and Jeane W. Anastas, "Breadwinners and Caregivers: Interviews with Working Women," *Journal of Gerontological Social Work* 14 (1989) (1/2), 19-40.

14. Elaine M. Brody, "Parent Care as a Normative Family Stress," *The Gerontologist* 25 (1985) (1), 19-29. Elaine M. Brody and Claire B. Schoonover, 1986. "Patterns of Parent-care When Adult Daughters Work and When They Do Not," *The Gerontologist* 26 (4), 372-81. Elaine M. Brody, et al., "Work Status and Parent Care: A Comparison of Four Groups of Women," *The Gerontologist* 27 (1987) (2), 201-8.

15. Eileen Manion, "Beauty Myth an Ugly Burden on Women," *Cleveland Plain Dealer*, 7 April, 1991.

16. Biddle, 82.

17. Julian Barling and Karyl E. MacEwen, "A Multitrait-multimethod Analysis of Four Maternal Employment Role Experiences," *Journal of Organizational Behavior* 9 (1988) (1), 344.

18. Esther R. Greenglass, Kaye-Lee Pantony, and Ronald J. Burke, "A Gender-role Perspective on Role Conflict, Work Stress and Social Support," in *Work and Family: Theory, Research, and Applications*, (Special issue), E. Goldsmith, (ed.), *Journal of Social Behavior and Personality* 3 (1988) (4), 317-28.

19. Jeffrey H. Greenhaus and Nicholas J. Beutell, "Sources of Conflict Between Work and Family Roles," *Academy of Management Review* 10 (1985) (1), 77.

20. Ronald J. Burke, "Some Antecedents and Consequences of Work-family Conflict," in "Work and Family: Theory, Research, and Applications," (Special issue), E. Goldsmith, (ed.), *Journal of Social Behavior and Personality* 3 (1988) (4), 287-302. Julian Barling, "Interrole Conflict and Marital Functioning Amongst Employed Fathers," *Journal of Occupational Behavior* 7 (January, 1986), 1-8. Brody, 1981.

21. Janet Dreyfus Gray, "The Married Professional Woman: An Examination of Her Role Conflicts and Coping Strategies," *Psychology of Women Quarterly* 7 (Spring, 1983), 235-43. Dorothy D. Nevill, "The Meaning of Work in Women's Lives: Role Conflict, Preparation, and Change," *The Counseling Psychologist* 12 (1984) (4), 131-33.

22. Debra Froberg, Dwenda Gjerdingen, and Marilyn Preston, "Multiple Roles and Women's Mental and Physical Health: What Have We Learned?" *Women and Health* 11 (Summer, 1986), 79-96.

23. Rosalind C. Barnett and Grace K. Baruch, "Women's Involvement in Multiple Roles and Psychological Distress," *Journal of Personality and Social Psychology* 49 (1985) (1), 135-45. Shelley Coverman, "Role Overload, Role Conflict, and Stress: Addressing Consequences of Multiple Role Demands" *Social Forces* 67 (June, 1989), 965-82. Rena L. Repetti, Karen A. Matthews, and Ingrid Waldron, "Employment and Women's Health: Effects of Paid Employment on Women's Mental and Physical

Health," *American Psychologist* 44 (November, 1989), 1394-1401. Angela Barron McBride, "Mental Health Effects of Women's Multiple Roles," *American Psychologist* 45 (March, 1990), 381-84.

24. Margaret L. Cassidy, "Role Conflict in the Postparental Period," *Research on Aging* 7 (September, 1985), 433-54.

25. Barnett and Baruch, 1985. Googins and Burden, 1987. Neal Krause, "Employment Outside the Home and Women's Psychological Well-being," *Social Psychiatry* 19 (1984), 41-8.

26. Ellen S. Amatea and Margaret L. Fong-Beyette, "Through a Different Lens: Examining Professional Women's Interrole Coping by Focus and Mode," *Sex Roles* 17 (1987) (5/6), 237-52.

27. Ibid.

28. Colleen P. O'Neill and Amos Zeichner, "Working Women: A Study of Relationships Between Stress, Coping and Health," *Journal of Obstetrics and Gynecology* 4(1985), 105-16. Charles J. Holahan, and Rudolf H. Moos, "Personality, Coping, and Family Resources in Stress Resistance: A Longitudinal Analysis," *Journal of Personality and Social Psychology* 51 (1986) (2), 389-95.

29. Arlie Hochschild, *The Second Shift* (New York: Avon Books, 1989). Amatea and Fong–Beyette, 1987. Ayala Pines and Ditsa Kafry, "The Experience of Tedium in Three Generations of Professional Women" *Sex Roles* 7 (1981) (2), 117-34. George V. Richard and Thomas S. Krieshok, "Occupational Stress, Strain, and Coping in University Faculty," *Journal of Vocational Behavior* 34 (February, 1989), 117-32.

30. Amatea and Fong–Beyette, 1987. Carole A. Rayburn, "Women and Stress: Some Implications for Therapy," *Women and Therapy* 5 (Summer/Fall, 1986), 239-47. Nancy C. Higgins, "Occupational Stress and Working Women: The Effectiveness of Two Stress Reduction Programs," *Journal of Vocational Behavior* 29 (August, 1986), 66-78. Mike L. McLaughlin, Sherilyn Cormier, and William H. Cormier, "Relation Between Coping Strategies and Distress, Stress, and Marital Adjustment of Multiple-role Women," *Journal of Counseling Psychology* 35 (1988) (2), 187-93.

31. Lucia Albino Gilbert and Vicki Rachlin, "Mental Health and Psychological Functioning of Dual-career Families," *The Counseling Psychologist* 15 (January, 1987), 7-49. Amatea and Fong–Beyette, 1987. Linn Spencer Hayes, "The Superwoman Myth," *Social Casework* 67 (September, 1986), 436-41. Sally A. Franek, "Cognitive Restructuring: A Program for Reentry Women," *Journal of College Student Personnel* 29 (November, 1985), 554-56.

32. Bonita C. Long, "Work-related Stress and Coping Strategies of Professional Women," *Journal of Employment Counseling* 25 (March, 1988), 37-44. Rayburn, 1986. Cynthia Fuchs Epstein, "The Politics of Stress: Public Visions, Private Realities," *The American Journal of Psychoanalysis* 45 (1985) (3), 282-90. Gilbert and Rachlin, 1987. Alexandra Cunningham and Graham S. Saayman, "Effective Functioning in Dual-career Families: An Investigation," *Journal of Family Therapy* 6 (November, 1984), 365-80. Hayes, 1986. Amatea and Fong–Beyette, 1987.

Sharon E. Robinson and Elizabeth K. Skarie, "Professional Women: Job Role Stresses and Psychosocial Variables," *American Mental Health Counselors Association Journal* 8 (July, 1986), 157-65.

33. McLaughlin et al., 1988. O'Neill and Zeichner, 1985.

34. Sandra Scarr, Deborah Phillips, and Kathleen McCartney, "Working Mothers and Their Families," *American Psychologist* 44 (November, 1989), 1402-9.

35. Schwartz, 1989. U.S. Dept. of Labor, 1989.

36. "Pay Gap Worrisome for Entire Nation," *Ravenna (Ohio) Record Courier,* 2 December, 1991, 4. Touchton and Davis, 1991.

37. *Administrative Compensation Survey,* (Washington, D.C.: College and University Personnel Association). Annual.

38. Popovich and Licata, 1987.

39. Charles C. Healy and Alice J. Welchert, "Mentoring Relations: A Definition to Advance Research and Practice," *Educational Researcher,* 19 (December, 1990), 17.

40. Mary Ann Danowitz Sagaria and Linda K. Johnsrud, "Generative Leadership," in *Empowering Women: Leadership Development Strategies on Campus,* Mary Ann Sagaria, (ed.), (San Francisco: Jossey-Bass, 1988), 13-26.

41. Melanie Suchet and Julian Barling, "Employed Mothers: Interrole Conflict, Spouse Support and Marital Functioning," *Journal of Occupational Behavior,* 7 (1986), 167-78.

42. Angela Barron McBride, "Multiple Roles and Depression," *Health Values,* 13 (March/April, 1989), 45-49. Donna L. Wiley, "The Relationship Between Work/Nonwork Role Conflict and Job-related Outcomes: Some Unanticipated Findings," *Journal of Management,* 13 (1987) (3), 467-72. Barnett and Baruch, 1985. Grace K. Baruch, Lois Biener, and Rosalind C. Barnett, "Women and Gender in Research on Work and Family Stress," *American Psychologist,* 42 (February, 1987), 130-36.

43. Karen A. Matthews and Judith Rodin, "Women's Changing Work Roles: Impact on Health, Family, and Public Policy," *American Psychologist,* 44 (November, 1989), 1389-93.

44. Brody, 1981.

Chapter 6. Women Administrators' Emerging Personal and Professional Concerns

1. Carol Shakeshaft, *Women in Educational Administration* (Newbury Park, CA: Sage Publications, 1987), 167.

2. Alice G. Sargent, *The Androgynous Manager,* (New York: American Management Association, 1982), 2.

3. Ibid., 17.

4. Ibid., 53.

5. Ibid., 55.

6. Virginia Ellen Schein, "The Relationship Between Sex-role Stereotypes and Requisite Management Characteristics," in *Journal of Applied Psychology*, Vol. 57, No. 2, (New York, April, 1973).

7. Kris K. Moore and Charlotte Decker Sutton, "Executive Women— Twenty Years Later," in *Harvard Business Review*, (New York, September-October, 1985), 42-66.

8. Ibid.

9. Karen M. Kearney and Laraine M. Roberts, "Building Your Vision Upon Principles of Educational Practice," in *California School Leadership Academy*, (San Rafael, CA, January, 1990), 1-6.

10. Thomas J. Sergiovanni, "Goals and Purposes of Schooling," in *"The Principalship" A Reflective Practice Perspective*, (Newton, M.A.: Allyn and Bacon, Inc., 1987). Thomas J. Sergiovanni, "Leadership and Excellence in Schooling," *Educational Leadership*, (New York, February, 1984), 4-13.

11. Patricia L. Freg, "How Do You Spell Success," *Entrepreneurial Woman*, Vol. 2, No. 9, (New York, November, 1991), 62-65.

12. Arleen Jacobson, *Women in Charge: Dilemmas of Women in Authority*, (New York: Van Nostrand Reinhold Company, 1985). Gayle Sato Stodder, "Girls Will/Won't Be Girls," *Entrepreneurial Woman*, Vol. 2, No. 7, (New York, September, 1991).

13. U.S. Department of Labor: Bureau of Labor Statistics, *Monthly Labor Review*, (New York, September, 1987).

14. Leslie Bennetts, "On Aggression in Politics: Are Women Judged By a Double Standard?," *New York Times*, (New York, February 12, 1979).

15. Martha G. Burrow, "Developing Women Managers: What Needs to Be Done?," *American Management Association Survey Report*, (New York, 1980).

16. Thomas J. Peters, "Symbols, Patterns, Settings: An Optimistic Case for Getting Things Done," *Organizational Dynamics*, (Autumn, 1978), 3-23.

17. National Institute of Business Management, Inc., "Finding the Right Mentor," *Working Smart*, Vol. 17, No. 17, (Alexandria, VA, November, 1991).

18. Margaret Hennig and Anne Jardim, "The Corporate Woman: How to Compete in a Man's World," *Mainliner*, (September, 1977), 33-106.

19. National Institute of Business Management, Inc., "Talking With Dorothy Sarnoff About Communicating," *Working Smart*, Vol. 17, No. 14, (Alexandria, VA, August 7, 1991). Arleen Jacobson, *Women in Charge: Dilemmas of Women in Authority*, (New York: Van Nostrand Reinhold Company, 1985).

20. Affirmative Action Office, "Sexual Harassment in the Workplace," (San Jose, CA, April 2, 1985).

21. Bob Weinstein, "Risky Business," *Entrepreneurial Woman*, (New York, May/June, 1990).

Chapter 7. Women and Mentoring in Higher Education

1. F.J. Lunding, G.I. Clements and D. S. Perkins, "Everyone Who Makes It Has a Mentor," *Harvard Business Review*, 56, (1978), 89-101. L. Jowers and K. Herr, "A Review of the Literature on Mentor-protege Relationships." *NLN Productions*, 15, (1990), 49-77. G.R. Roche, "Much Ado About Mentors," *Harvard Business Review*, 57, (1979), 14-28. J.G. Clawson, *Superior-subordinate Relationships in Management Development.* Unpublished doctoral dissertation. Harvard University. (1979). G.W. Dalton, P.H. Thompson and R.L. Price, "The Four Stages of Professional Careers—A New Look at Performance by Professionals," *Organizational Dynamics*, 6 (1987) (1), 19-42. M. Queralt, *The Role of the Mentor in Career Development of University Faculty Members and Academic Administrators.* Unpublished doctoral dissertation. University of Miami.

2. E.B. Bolton, "A Conceptual Analysis of the Mentor Relationship in Career Development of Women," *Adult Education*, 30 (1980), 195-207.

3. C.F. Epstein, *Woman's Place: Options and Limits in Professional Careers.* (California: University of California Press, 1971).

4. R. Williams and R. Blackburn, "Mentoring and Junior Faculty Productivity," *Journal of Nursing Education*, 27 (5) (1988), 204-209.

5. M. Henning and A. Jardim, *The Managerial Women*, (New York: Anchor Press/Doubleday, 1977).

6. Ibid.

7. C.D. Orth and F. Jacobs, "Women in Management: Pattern for Change," *Harvard Business Review*, 49, (1971), 139-147.

8. Henning and Jardim, 1977.

9. Epstein, 131.

10. D. Levinson, *The Seasons of a Man's Life*, (New York: Alfred A. Knopf, 1978). Rosabeth M. Kanter, *Men and Women of the Corporation*, (New York: Basic Books, 1977), 181-84.

11. Kanter, 1977 and Epstein, 1971.

12. Kanter, 1977.

13. K.M. Moore, "The Role of Mentors in Developing Leaders for Academe," *Educational Record*, 63, (1982), 22-28.

14. Ibid.

15. D. Levinson, "Growing up With a Dream," *Psychology Today*, 11, (1977), 20-34.

Chapter 8. Environmental and Social Factors

1. J. Atkinson, *An Introduction to Motivation*, (Cambridge, MA: Van Nostrand Co., 1964). National Manpower Council, *Womanpower*, (New York: Columbia University Press, 1957).

2. J. Atkinson and D. McClelland, *The Achieving Society*, (New York: Van Nostrand Co., 1961). R. Taylor, "Personality Traits and Discrepant Achievements: A Review," *Journal of Counseling Psychology*, 11, (1980), 76-82.

3. J. Lysman-Blumen, "How Ideology Shapes Women's Lives," *Scientific American*, 226, 34-42. B. Dill, "The Dialectics of Black Womanhood," *Journal of Women in Culture and Society*, 4, (1979), 58-64.

4. M. Komarovsky, "Cultural Contradictions and Sex Roles," *American Journal of Sociology*, (1946), 184-189.

5. E. Haskins, *Women and Jobs*, (Career Planning Center, Washington, D.C., 1986). E. Bardwick, *Readings on the Psychology of Women*, (New York: Harper and Row Publishers, Inc., 1972).

6. E. Bardwick, *Readings on the Psychology of Women*. W. Nables, "Extended Self: Breaking the So-Called Negro Self-Concept," *The Journal of Black Psychology*, 2, (1976), 16. J. Ladner, "The Black Woman Today," *Ebony*, 12, (1977), 5.

7. R. Silverstein, *Children of the Dark Ghetto*, (New York: Praeger). W. Nables, "Extended Self," 2, 16.

8. J. Conway, "Woman Reformers and American Cultures," *Journal of Social History*, 5, (1972), 164-177. Horner, *The Motive to Avoid Success and Changing Aspirations of College Women*, Women on Campus, a Symposium, 1970.

9. Atkinson and McClelland, *The Achieving Society*.

10. Bardwick, *Readings on the Psychology of Women*.

Chapter 9. Questioning the System

1. Anne Wilson Schaef, *Women's Reality*, (San Francisco: Harper & Row Publications, 1985).

2. Jaclyn Fierman, "Why Women Still Don't Hit The Top," *Fortune*, Vol. 122, (1990, July 30), 41-62.

3. Carol Goldberg, Aileen Gorman and Kathleen Hansen, "Issues in the Corporate Workplace," *New England Journal of Public Policy*, 6, (1990), 65-73.

4. Sherry N. Penney and Nancy Kelly, "Why Not a Fifty-Fifty Goal? Increasing Female Leadership," *New England Journal of Public Policy*, 6, (1990), 39-46.

5. Marcia Dohrman, "Why Women are Underrepresented in Administrative Positions: A Review of the Research," (ED 247868), 1982.

6. Nina Gupta, *Barriers to the Advancement of Women in Educational Administration: Sources and Remedies*. Prepared for the Women's Leadership Project, sponsored by the American Association of School Administrators as part of Project AWARE, (New York, NY: Ford Foundation, 1983).

7. Matina Horner, "The Changing Challenge: From Double Bind to Double Burden," *New England Journal of Public Policy*, 6, (1990), 39-46.

8. Suzanne Skevington and Deborah Baker, (eds.) *The Social Identity of Women*, (Newbury Park, CA: Sage Publications, 1989).

9. Rosabeth M. Kanter, *Men and Women of the Corporation*, (New York: Basic Books, Inc., 1977).

10. Claire M. Reuzetti and Daniel J. Curran, *Women, Men and Society*, (Needham Heights, MA: Allyn and Bacon, 1989).

11. Carol S. Pearson, Donna L. Shavlik, and Judith G. Touchton, *Educating the Majority*, (New York: MacMillan Publishing Company, 1989).

Chapter 10. Communication Strategies for Women

1. Diana Pounder, "The Gender Gap in Salaries of Educational Administration Professors," *Education Administration Quarterly*, 25, no. 2, (May, 1989), 15.

2. Debra Blum, "Environment Still Hostile to Women in Academe, New Evidence Indicates," *Chronicle of Higher Education*, (October 9, 1991), 1.

3. Barbara Sylvia, "Promoting Equality for Women in Academe," *Planning for Higher Education*, 19, (1991), 46.

4. Annie L. Cotten-Huston, "Gender Communications," in *Human Communication as a Field of Study*, Sarah Sanderson King (ed.), (New York: State University of New York Press, 1989), 129.

5. Deborah Tannen, *You Just Don't Understand: Women and Men in Conversation*, (New York: Ballantine Books, 1990).

6. J.J. Speizer, "The Administrative Skills Program: What Have We Learned?," *New Directions for Higher Education: Women in Higher Education Administration*, 45, (1984).

7. R. W. Rebore, *Educational Administration: A Management Approach*, (New Jersey: Prentice Hall, 1985), 174.

8. Charlotte Epstein and Cliff L. Wood, "Women in Community College Administration," *Community and Junior College Journal*, 55, no. 2, (1984), 21.

9. Rowland G. Baughman, "Organizational Communication," in *Human Communication as a Field of Study*, Sarah Sanderson King (ed.), (New York: State University of New York Press, 1989), 146.

10. Flora Ida Oritz and Catherine Marshall, "Women in Educational Administration," in *Handbook of Research on Educational Administration*, Norman J. Boyan (ed.), (New York: Longman, 1988).

11. Ernest G. Bormann and Nancy C. Bormann, *Effective Small Group Communication*, (Minneapolis: Burgess Publishing, 1988), 129.

12. Ibid., 136.

13. M.E. Johnson and C. Brems, "Differences in Interpersonal Functioning as Related to Sex-role Orientation," *Psychology: A Journal of Human Behavior*, 26, no. 4, (1989), 50.

14. K.J. Gruber and J. Gaebelein, "Sex Differences in Listening Comprehension," *Sex Roles*, 5, no. 3, (1979), 300.

15. Constance Courtney Staley and Jerry L. Cohen, "Communicator Style and Social Style: Similarities and Differences Between the Sexes," *Communication Quarterly*, 36, no. 3, (1988), 200.

16. Bormann and Bormann, 133.

17. V.E. Wheeless and C. Berryman-Fink, "Perceptions of Women Managers and Their Communicator Competencies," *Communication Quarterly*, 33, no. 2, (1985), 145.

18. Ronald B. Adler and George Rodman, *Understanding Human Communication*, (Florida: Holt, Rinehart & Winston, 1991), 26.

19. D.C. Baker, "A Qualitative and Quantitative Analysis of Verbal Style and the Elimination of Potential Leaders in Small Groups," *Communication Quarterly*, 38, no. 1, (1990), 25.

20. E. Mark Hanson, *Educational Administration and Organizational Behavior*, (Boston: Allyn & Bacon, 1985), 183.

21. Bonita C. Long, "Sex-Role Orientation, Coping Strategies, and Self-Efficacy of Women in Traditional and Nontraditional Occupations," *Psychology of Women Quarterly*, 13, (1989), 321.

22. Adler and Rodman, 69.

23. R. Taiibi, "Words Between the Sexes," *TWA Ambassador*, (September, 1990), 68.

24. Tannen, 85.

25. Carole Spitzack and Kathryn Carter, "Women in Communication Studies: A Typology for Revision," *The Quarterly Journal of Speech*, 73, no. 4, (1987), 413.

26. Adler and Rodman, 72.

27. J.J. Bradac and A. Mulac, "A Molecular View of Powerful and Powerless Speech Styles: Attributional Consequences of Specific Language Features and Communicator Intentions," *Communication Monographs*, 51, (1984), 317.

28. Adler and Rodman, 85.

29. Ibid., 86.

30. Spitzack and Carter, 401-423.

31. Phoebe Lambert, "Women into Educational Management," *Adults Learning*, 1, no. 4, (1989), 106.

32. Tannen, 122.

33. Wendy Martyna, "What Does 'He' Mean?" *Journal of Communication*, 28, (1978), 138.

34. Karen Johnson, *Listener Characteristics and the Measurement of Listening* (unpublished masters thesis, University of Northern Colorado, 1988).

35. Gruber and Gaebelein, 308.

36. George Duerst-Lahti, "But Women Play the Game Too: Communication Control and Influence in Administrative Decision Making," *Administration & Society*, 22, no. 2, (1990), 201.

37. Charol Shakeshaft, "The Gender Gap in Research in Educational Administration," *Educational Administration Quarterly*, 25, no. 4, (1989), 329.
38. M.A. Morris, *A Review of Research on Feedback*, (unpublished manuscript, 1988).
39. Cotten-Huston, 132.
40. Tannen, 1990.
41. L.R. Robinson and H.T. Reis, "The Effects of Interruption, Gender and Status on Interpersonal Perceptions," *Journal of Nonverbal Behavior*, 13, no. 3, (1989), 151.
42. Cotten-Huston, 132.
43. Ibid., 133.
44. Rebore, 174.
45. Tannen, 15.
46. Ibid., 16.
47 Lambert, 107.
48. Blum, 21.
49. K.M. Moore, "Careers in College and University Administration: How are Women Affected?" *New Directions for Higher Education: Women in Higher Education Administration*, 45, (1984).
50. Baughman, 137.
51. Tannen, 118.
52. Baughman, 149.
53. Ibid.
54. Tannen, 150.
55. Nona Lyons, "Visions and Competencies: An Educational Agenda for Exploring the Ethical and Intellectual Dimensions of Decision-Making and Conflict Negotiation" in *Changing Education: Women as Radicals and Conservators*, Joyce Antler and Sari Knopp Biklen (eds.), (New York: State University of New York Press, 1990).
56. Ibid.
57. Tannen, 181.
58. Long, 321.
59. Charlotte Hanna, "The Organizational Context for Affirmative Action for Women Faculty," *Journal of Higher Education*, 59, no. 4, (1988), 399.
60. Craig Richards, "The Search for Equity in Educational Administration," in *Handbook of Research on Educational Administration*, Norman J. Boyan (ed.), (New York: Longman, 1988), 160.
61. Sylvia, 44.
62. Roger Rosenblatt, "Sexual Bigotry," *Life*, 14, no. 16, (1991), 33.
63. Duerst-Lahti, 202.

Chapter 11. Power and Politics: The Leadership Challenge

1. John Naisbitt and Patricia Aburdene, "The 1990s: Decade of Women in Leadership," *Megatrends 2000: 10 New Directions for the 1990s,* (New York: Avon Books, 1990), 228-256.
2. Lee G. Bolman and Terrence E. Deal, *Modern Approaches to Understanding and Managing Organizations,* (San Francisco: Jossey-Bass Publishers, 1984), 109.
3. Ibid., 26.
4. John W. Gardner, *On Leadership,* (New York: The Free Press: A Division of MacMillan, Inc., 1990), 55.
5. Ibid., 66.
6. Ibid., 109.
7. Bolman and Deal, 133.
8. Alvin Toffler, *Power Shift: Knowledge, Wealth, and Violence at the Edge of the 21st Century,* (New York: Bantam Books, 1990), 9.
9. Ibid., 17.
10. Ibid., 16.
11. Estelle R. Ramey, (in her presidential address to the annual meeting of the Association of Women in Science, Georgetown University School of Medicine).
12. "The New Agenda for Women in Higher Education," (Washington D.C.: American Council on Education, 1988), 1.
13. Study of Fortune 1000 Companies, (Office of Federal Contract Compliance Programs: Washington, D.C., 1990).
14. Nancy Hensel, "Realizing Gender Equality in Higher Education," (ASHE ERIC Education Report, 1991), 2.
15. Sally Helgesen, *The Female Advantage: Women's Ways of Leadership,* (New York: Doubleday, 1990), 253-259.
16. M. Loden, *Feminine Leadership or How to Succeed in Business Without Being One of the Boys,* (New York: Time Books, 1985).
17. Jinx Melia, *Breaking into the Boardroom: What Every Woman Needs to Know,* (New York: G.P. Putnam's Sons, 1986), 13-25.
18. Ibid., 13-25.
19. "Women and Their Power," *Washington Post,* (May 19, 1988), E5.
20. CBS Winter Olympics, Television Interview of Scot Hamilton, February 24, 1992.
21. Michael Korda, *Success: How Every Man and Woman Can Achieve It,* (New York: Random House, 1977), 13-45. Toffler, 15-16, 238-240.
22. Carol S. Pearson, *Awakening the Heros Within,* (Harper San Francisco: A Division of Harper Collins, Publishers, 1991).
23. Ibid., 7-12.
24. John J. Gabarro and John P. Kotter, "Managing Your Boss," *Harvard Business Review,* Reprint No. 80104, (January-February, 1980), 92-99.
25. Bolman and Deal, 250-255.

26. Anita J. Harrow and Barbara Holmes, "Developing Women Leaders for the 21st Century: Agenda for Change," (adapted from a presentation at the annual convention of the American Association of Community and Junior Colleges, in Las Vegas, Nevada, April, 1988).

27. M. Scott Peck, *The Road Less Traveled*, (New York: Touchstone Book, published by Simon and Schuster, 1978), 16-18.

28. Alinsky, in Bolman and Deal, (1984), 109.

29. Gardner, 181.

30. "The Backlash Debate," *Time*, (March 9, 1992), 55.

Chapter 12. Empowerment: The Politics of Change

1. Peter Block, *The Empowered Manager: Positive Political Skills at Work*, (San Francisco: Jossey-Bass, 1989), 66.

2. Eileen "Sage" Bennet, "Self-empowerment for Women: Going Beyond the Stereotypes," *Herizons*, (Spring Edition, 1992), 1.

3. Douglas E. Mitchell and William G. Spady, "Authority and Power, and the Legitimation of Social Control," *Educational Administration Quarterly*, V. 19, No. 1, (Winter, 1983), 5-33.

4. Websters 3rd World Dictionary, (1957).

5. Random House Dictionary, 2nd Edition, (1987).

6. Warren Bennis, "Transformative Power," *Leadership and Organizational Culture*, (1990), Chapter 4, 64-71.

7. Carol Jacklin, Lecture: "Cognitive Differences Between Men and Women," California Lutheran University, Colloquium of Scholars, (May, 1989).

8. Virginia Sapiro, *The Political Integration of Woman*, (1990).

9. Nina J. Easton, "I'm Not a Feminist, But...," *Los Angeles Times Magazine*, (February, 1992), 16.

10. Ibid.

11. Nancy L. Kassebaum in Easton, (1992), 15.

12. Linda R. Silver, "Deference to Authority in the Feminized Professions," *School Library Journal*, (January, 1988), 21-28.

13. Barbara Myerhoff and Elinor Lenz, *The Feminization of America*, (Los Angeles: Jeremy Tarcher, 1985).

14. Easton, (1992).

15. Paula Morrison, "A Shot in the Dark: Tracking Hate Crimes by Gender is Commendable but Will it Save Any Lives?," *Los Angeles Times Magazine*, (March, 1992).

16. Carole Pateman, *The Disorder of Women: Democracy, Feminism and Political Theory*, (Cambridge: Polity Press, 1989), 118-140.

17. Jean Beth Elshtain, *Public Man, Private Woman*, (Princeton: Princeton University Press, 1981), 299-353.

18. Pipa Norris, *Politics and Sexual Equality*, (Sussex: Wheatsheaf Books Ltd. 1987), 76.

19. Bruce Romanish, *Empowering Teachers: Restructuring Schools for the 21st Century*, (New York: University Press of America, 1991), 5.

20. Diane Dunlop and Goldman, "Rethinking Power in Schools," *Educational Administration Quarterly*, Vol. 27, No. 1, (1991), 5-29.

21. R.J.S. "Mac" Macpherson, "Talking Up and Justifying Organization: The Creation and Control of Knowledge About Being Organized." *Studies in Educational Administration*, 41 (Armidale: University of New England, May, 1986).

22. Block, (1989), 32.

23. John G. Mitchell, *Re-envisioning Educational Leadership: A Phenomenological Approach*, (New York: Garland Publishing, 1990).

24. Myra Sadker, David Sadker and Susan Klein, "The Role of Administrator Training in Developing Equity Knowledge and Skills," in *Review of Research in Education*, Gerald Grant (ed.), (Washington, D.C.: American Educational Research Association, 1991, Book 17), 290.

25. Sadker, (1991), 284-288.

26. Sapiro, (1990).

27. Richard Prawatt, "Conversations with Self and Settings: A Framework for Thinking About Teacher Empowerment," *American Educational Research Journal*, 4, (Winter, 1991), 737-757.

28. Robert Frost, *Complete Poems of Robert Frost*, (New York: Holt, Rinehart and Winston, 1962), "Mending Wall," 47.

29. Nancy A. Scott and Sue Spooner, "Women Administrators: Stressors and Strategies," *Initiatives*, (1991), 31-36.

30. Sharon Kinsella, in Easton, (1992).

31. Judith G. Touchton and Lynne Davis, *Fact Book on Women in Higher Education*, American Council on Education, (New York: MacMillan, 1991), 16.

32. Bolman and Deal, 20-21, in Baldridge, 1971.

33. Sapiro, (1990), 13.

34. Robert Frost, 1962.

DATE DUE

JUN 1 5 1999		
ILL 84753117 5/4/00		
AG 25 '03		
OC 20 03		